LOOKING FOR LINCOLN IN ILLINOIS

LOOKING FOR LINCOLN IN ILLINOIS

HISTORIC HOUSES OF LINCOLN'S ILLINOIS

Erika Holst

Southern Illinois University Press
Carbondale

Southern Illinois University Press
www.siupress.com

Copyright © 2018 by the Looking for Lincoln Heritage Coalition
Printed in the United States of America

21 20 19 18   4 3 2 1

Publication of this book has been made possible by the generous
support of the Looking for Lincoln Heritage Coalition, courtesy
of Sarah Watson, executive director.

Cover illustrations (clockwise from top): Abraham Lincoln, 1857,
courtesy of the Abraham Lincoln Presidential Library and
the Illinois Historic Preservation Agency (ALPL/IHPA); state
outline by Tom Willcockson; Lincoln Home National Historic
Site, Springfield, courtesy of the ALPL/IHPA; Carl Sandburg's
Galesburg birthplace as it appeared in the 1890s, courtesy of the
ALPL/IHPA; home of Dr. Richard Eels, Quincy, courtesy of
the Historical Society of Quincy and Adams County; home of
Governor John Wood, Quincy, courtesy of the ALPL/IHPA.

Library of Congress Cataloging-in-Publication Data
Names: Holst, Erika, author.
Title: Looking for Lincoln in Illinois : historic houses of Lincoln's
Illinois / Erika Holst.
Description: Carbondale : Southern Illinois University Press, 2018.
| Includes bibliographical references and index.
Identifiers: LCCN 2018005132 | ISBN 9780809336968
(paperback) | ISBN 9780809336975 (ebook)
Subjects: LCSH: Lincoln, Abraham, 1809–1865—Homes and
haunts—Illinois—Guidebooks. | Historic sites—Illinois—
Guidebooks. | Illinois—Buildings, structures, etc.—Guidebooks.
| BISAC: TRAVEL / Museums, Tours, Points of Interest. | TRAVEL
/ United States / Midwest / East North Central (IL, IN, MI,
OH, WI). | HISTORY / United States / State & Local / Midwest
(IA, IL, IN, KS, MI, MN, MO, ND, NE, OH, SD, WI).
| ARCHITECTURE / Historic Preservation / General.
Classification: LCC E457.64 .H65 2018 | DDC 977.3—dc23
LC record available at https://lccn.loc.gov/2018005132

To my parents, who set me on a path
to following my dreams.

I miss you every day.

CONTENTS

FOREWORD

*Here I have lived a quarter of a century and have passed from a
young to an old man.*
—Abraham Lincoln, February 11, 1861

FEW AMERICANS HAVE DEMONSTRATED THE COMBINATION OF
ambition and selflessness, integrity and pragmatism, confidence and humility, and persistent pursuit of what is right that Abraham Lincoln did. Where
did he get the qualities and skills it took to steer the nation and democracy
through the crisis of the Civil War?

The major portion of Lincoln's training for this task took place in central
Illinois. Little has been written about his life and development from the time
he arrived in Illinois at age 21 until his departure for the White House over 31
years later. The frontier of central Illinois was the perfect place for this raw-boned farmhand to hone his natural talent and intellectual skills to meet the
challenges that he would face as the leader of the nation.

Lincoln and central Illinois evolved on parallel courses, maturing together.
The coming of the railroads some 20 years after his arrival totally altered
the region. He learned to deal with change as he experienced the revolutionary transformation of society that took place there in the 1850s. He traveled
extensively throughout the region, first by horse and then by train, practicing
law and pursuing politics. There are numerous sites, buildings, homes, street-scapes, and landscapes that still exist in the towns he visited and the prairies
he crossed. This region felt the presence and influence of Lincoln. It, in turn,
influenced and molded him.

An in-depth understanding of Lincoln cannot be reached without becoming acquainted with the region and Lincoln's role in it. Illinois became a key
state in the 1850s, and central Illinois was the state's most vital area. Lincoln
gained the Republican nomination for president because he built the network
to do so while traveling and working in central Illinois.

The Abraham Lincoln National Heritage Area was created by Congress
in 2008 as part of the National Park Service. The 42-county region preserves
the life and times of Lincoln in central Illinois. The nationally significant

landscape is filled with numerous Lincoln sites from his pre-presidential life. The Looking for Lincoln Heritage Coalition coordinates projects, programs, and events that focus on the unique stories of the area; enhances and promotes Lincoln scholarship and heritage tourism; and stimulates economic development within the region.

This volume is the fourth in a series of books examining Lincoln's development and rise in central Illinois. It is our intent that these publications will augment the Looking for Lincoln Heritage Coalition's efforts to

- create engaging experiences that connect places and stories throughout the Heritage Area and promote awareness of the region's history, culture, and significance;
- stimulate tourism that supports increased economic activity and investment in heritage resources; and
- raise public consciousness about the benefits of preserving the historical and cultural legacies of central Illinois.

It is our hope that you are inspired to learn more about the life, times, and legacy of Abraham Lincoln in central Illinois and the people, places, and forces in the region that shaped and elevated him to the White House.

Board of Directors
Daniel Noll, Chair
Looking for Lincoln Heritage Coalition

ACKNOWLEDGMENTS

IT HAS BEEN MY PROFESSIONAL DREAM TO WRITE A BOOK

about the historic houses of Illinois since my college days, when I was an intern at the David Davis Mansion State Historic Site, in Bloomington. It was always something I had in the back of my mind, but as way led on to way in my career (to paraphrase Robert Frost), the idea went nowhere for a long time.

Flash forward twenty years, when Sarah Watson, the executive director of the Looking for Lincoln Heritage Coalition, contacted me about writing a book on historic houses for their Looking for Lincoln in Illinois series. What followed was more than a year of visiting fascinating places, often with my family in tow, and late nights tapping away at my laptop to produce the volume you are now holding. The entire process, start to finish, was a dream come true.

My thanks go to many people. First and foremost are Sarah Watson and the book committee of the Looking for Lincoln Heritage Coalition, who extended the opportunity to write this book and provided support and encouragement along the way. At Looking for Lincoln, Heather Wickens gave me her input and Jeanette Cowden kept everything running smoothly on the business end of things. Bryon Andreasen, a member of the book committee as well as a historian at the Latter-day Saints Church History Museum, reviewed my chapter on the Joseph Smith Homestead and Mansion House.

Most of the historical images in this book come from the Abraham Lincoln Presidential Museum's unparalleled collection of 19th-century Illinois photographs. Samuel Wheeler, the Illinois state historian, kindly approved and facilitated the use of these images; James Cornelius, Lincoln curator, and Jennifer Ericson, Lincoln photographs associate (since retired), promptly and thoroughly assisted me in locating and reproducing Lincoln-related images; and Roberta Fairburn, photographs assistant in the audiovisual department, helped in locating historic images and then digitized them.

Several historic images throughout the book were drawn from other museums and repositories. Robert Evans of the Pittsfield Historical Society; Benjamin Pollard of the Bryant Cottage State Historic Site; Joey Woolridge of the DeWitt County Museum; Jean Kay of the Historical Society of Quincy and Adams County; Wendy Wilder of the Vermilion County Museum; Matthew Souther of the Abraham Lincoln Library and Museum at Lincoln Memorial

University; and Christopher Schnell of the Archives/Special Collections at the University of Illinois-Springfield kindly assisted in locating and accessing images from their historic collections.

In visiting nearly two dozen historic houses over the course of a year, I have come to realize that the people who work at historic sites are treasures every bit as much as the sites themselves are. These people give their time and energy, often on a volunteer basis, to share a site's story for the enrichment of visitors and the community at large. The collective knowledge held by these dedicated interpreters is staggering, and I am grateful to everyone who shared that knowledge with me as I worked on this book: Lorraine McCallister at the Reddick Mansion in Ottawa; Marilyn Ayers at the Bryant Cottage State Historic Site in Bement (since retired); Joey Woolridge at the C. H. Moore Homestead in Clinton; Joanne Forrest and Kay Nims at the Oglesby Mansion in Decatur; Don Richardson and Lachlan Mackay at the Joseph Smith Homestead and Mansion House in Nauvoo; Emily McInerney and Dan Hirst at the Trobaugh-Good House in Decatur; Laura Chamberlain at the William Watson Hotel in Pittsfield; Reg Ankrom at the John Wood Mansion in Quincy; Julian Mackenzie at the Richard Eells House in Quincy; Sue Richter and Wendy Wilder at the Vermilion County Museum in Danville; Jerry Smith at the Broadwell Inn in Pleasant Plains; Linda Garvert at the Iles House in Springfield; Jennifer Caldwell at the Vachel Lindsay Home State Historic Site in Springfield; Terry Jones at Lincoln's New Salem State Historic Site in Petersburg; and Christie Hill Russell, Chuck Hand, Greg McHenry, and Susan Stafford at the Milton K. Alexander House in Paris.

I would like to single out a few people for the extra help they provided. Lorraine McCallister not only shared information about the Reddick Mansion but also facilitated the acquisition of historical images. Likewise Jeff Saulsbery at the David Davis Mansion State Historic Site; Tim Townsend, Susan Haake, and John Popolis at the Lincoln Home National Historic Site; and Lachlan Mackay of the Joseph Smith Homestead and Mansion House provided digital images of modern views of their sites. Brian Wielt shared research about the Trobaugh-Good House. Jane Ann Petty provided extra information about the William Watson Hotel. Reg Ankrom generously let me tag along on a private tour of the John Wood Mansion he was giving his grandchildren. John Cornell graciously gave me permission to take photographs at the Richard Eells house, as did Justin Blandford at the Vachel Lindsay Home State Historic Site. Jerry Smith gave up part of his Saturday to make a special trip to the Broadwell Inn to give me a tour during the off-season; and Linda Garvert gave me a tour of the Iles House during the off-season as well.

My former colleagues at the Springfield Art Association were more than just coworkers; they are my friends and "work family." Thank you to Betsy Dollar, Erin Svendsen, Charlotte Kane, Mary Beth Burke, Corrin McWhirter, and Jan Arnold for being such wonderful people to be around and for always cheering me on.

Finally, I thank my family for their unfailing love and support as I researched and wrote this book. Many a weekend over the past year was spent piling into the family car and taking off through the cornfields to visit historic sites. My husband, Chris Schnell, a historian himself, often forewent the privilege of going on tours so he could wrangle our small son, Anders, who usually preferred a trip to the local playground. My stepson Adam, on the other hand, is a budding history buff who thoroughly enjoyed his visits to the sites. On the whole, we made a lot of great family memories on these road trips through Illinois. The "Schnell boys" are my home and my heart.

Erika Holst

LOOKING FOR LINCOLN IN ILLINOIS

Circled numbers show locations of the 22 historic houses of Lincoln's Illinois.

INTRODUCTION

In the 30 years Lincoln lived in Illinois, his family, military service, law practice, and political aspirations took him all over the state, from Galena in the northwest to Cairo at the southern tip, and most of the counties in between.

Lincoln's Illinois was a place of unbroken prairie, of steamboats and railroads, of new settlers' log cabins and bustling county seats. The physical geography of Lincoln's world has long since given way to a modern one of interstates and commercial farmland and cities. Yet, scattered throughout Illinois, houses and inns from Lincoln's time survive. These structures each have unique stories to tell about Lincoln, his friends, and his world.

This book is a guide to 22 historic houses of Lincoln's Illinois. The featured sites have been organized into three groups: Lincoln and Family includes places where Lincoln or his family members resided. Lincoln's Friends and Colleagues includes the homes of Lincoln's acquaintances and professional associates. Lincoln's Times and Legacy includes sites that illuminate Lincoln's lifetime or legacy. All of the 22 houses profiled are in the 42 counties in central Illinois designated as the Abraham Lincoln National Heritage Area. With two exceptions, all are open to the public as historic sites available to tour (the exceptions, a hotel and an art center, welcome visitors interested in learning about Lincoln). The profile of each site in this book explores its history and connection to Lincoln and highlights exceptional features or objects that modern-day visitors can expect to see; these profiles are illustrated with a mix of historical and modern photographs.

In addition, the book includes a section titled "Related Lincoln Sites." These are sites with a strong connection to Lincoln or his times that are not necessarily open to the public, yet may be of interest to travelers who wish to drive by.

The hope is that those who read this book will be inspired to visit these historic treasures in person. Each of them is a physical link to Lincoln's life and legacy; each of them is a doorway to greater understanding about the man and his times.

Be sure to check with each site before visiting to determine hours and admission fees.

PART 1. LINCOLN AND FAMILY

The sites described in this section are the last surviving structures in the state where Abraham Lincoln or members of his family lived. Lincoln was known to have boarded or resided in at least a half-dozen different houses during his tenure in Illinois; his vast network of in-laws and step-relations had at least a half-dozen more houses among them. Only two remain: the Lincoln Home National Historic Site and the Vachel Lindsay Home State Historic Site. Two more sites in this section, the Second Lincoln-Berry Store and the Lincoln Log Cabin State Historic Site, are reproductions of buildings no longer extant.

Lincoln's rise from a poor working-class individual to an urban gentleman is richly illustrated by visits to these sites. Lincoln himself lived at two of them: the Second Lincoln-Berry Store, at Lincoln's New Salem State Historic Site, and his house on Eighth and Jackson Streets in Springfield (the only home he ever owned). At the former, 24-year-old Lincoln slept in the rear of the two-room store that was his faltering means of making a living. He had few personal possessions and scarcely an idea of where his life would ultimately lead him. At the latter, Lawyer Lincoln supported his family in refined middle-class style in a spacious dwelling decorated with carpets, wallpaper, and mahogany furniture.

Likewise, the home of Lincoln's father, Thomas, at Lincoln Log Cabin State Historic Site vividly illustrates the humble background from which Lincoln rose. Lincoln never lived there himself, but the two-room cabin is similar to (indeed, bigger than) the cabins Lincoln grew up in. At the end of his life, Thomas Lincoln was sharing a small cabin with whitewashed walls and bare floors with ten other individuals.

Over in Springfield, meanwhile, Clark and Ann Smith were living in a genteel frame house with walnut trim. Ann was Mary Lincoln's younger sister; her husband, Clark, was a prosperous merchant who would grow very wealthy during the course of his lifetime. Lincoln, who once described himself as a "friendless, uneducated, penniless boy," eventually became a gentleman of "pride, wealth, and aristocratic family distinction." A visit to the Smith house (now the Vachel Lindsay Home State Historic Site) allows viewers to see the social setting to which upwardly mobile young men like Lincoln aspired and which he ultimately achieved.

1. SECOND LINCOLN-BERRY STORE

The Second Lincoln-Berry Store has been meticulously reconstructed to its 1830s appearance using archival and archaeological evidence.

Visit the Second Lincoln-Berry Store at Lincoln's New Salem State Historic Site, 15588 History Lane, Petersburg.

ABRAHAM LINCOLN SPENT SIX OF THE MOST FORMATIVE

years of his life in the small village of New Salem. When he arrived at age 22, he was a penniless young man without a profession. When he left at age 28, he was a newly minted lawyer and a successful politician. Along the way, he took on a number of odd jobs to get by. One of those jobs was storekeeping in partnership with William F. Berry.

Lincoln moved to New Salem in 1831 to work as a clerk in the store of Denton Offut, but that store failed within a year. In the spring of 1832, the Black Hawk War broke out, and Lincoln enlisted in the Illinois state militia. When his term of service ended in July, Lincoln found himself, as he put it, "without means and out of business" with "nothing elsewhere to go to." Fate stepped in when Rowan Herndon offered to sell out his share of a local general store to Lincoln in exchange for a promissory note of payment.

In August 1832 Lincoln began keeping store with 21-year-old Berry, who had also purchased an interest in the business. Their establishment started in a three-room building south of New Salem's main street (the "First Lincoln-Berry Store"). In January 1833 they bought out the stock of Reuben Radford's store (again on credit) and moved into his building (the "Second Lincoln-Berry Store"). This new store had a large front room where the merchandise was displayed and a back room where Lincoln slept.

Stores were local gathering places, and Lincoln reportedly enjoyed the social aspects of storekeeping. Farmers often idled away the hours swapping stories and talking politics in the local store while their grain was ground and their wool carded. Because merchants were in the thick of social and political activity in town, they were often viewed as community leaders, a distinction Lincoln also likely enjoyed.

What Lincoln didn't seem to enjoy, or at least take to, was the actual business of running a store, preferring instead to socialize when the store was full of people and to read books when it wasn't. In a time when purchases were typically made on credit or by barter, Lincoln and Berry did not collect money or goods fast enough to pay their bills as they came due. Eventually, as Lincoln put it, the store "winked out." He sold his interest to Berry, who in turn sold out a year later.

After his experiment as a merchant failed, Lincoln supported himself by surveying and by drawing up the occasional legal document for residents of

Lincoln liked the social aspects of storekeeping but lacked the will or the aptitude to be a successful merchant.

the town. This income was supplemented by pay drawn as a state representative and by his appointment as the postmaster of New Salem; this assemblage of work allowed him to get by and not much more. When Berry died in 1835, Lincoln found himself on the hook for the entirety of the debt they had taken on during their storekeeping days. The sum, which has been estimated at $1,100, was so enormous that Lincoln referred to it as his "national debt."

The town of New Salem was already starting to wane by the time Lincoln left for Springfield in 1837. In 1839 nearby Petersburg was named the seat of Menard County, and within a year New Salem was all but deserted. By 1866 a single log cabin was all that remained of the once-thriving town; a few years later, that too was gone.

The legend of Lincoln's time in the town persisted, however, and the site, though abandoned, was never forgotten. Newspaper magnate William Randolph Hearst was so taken by Lincoln's connection to the site that he purchased it in 1906 and conveyed it in trust to the Old Salem Chautauqua Association. Interest in New Salem grew with the Illinois Centennial celebration of 1918, and that year the Chautauqua Association donated the village site to the state of Illinois with the hope that the state would one day reconstruct the village. In 1932 work began on rebuilding the village's original buildings on their original foundations. From 1934 to 1941, this work was carried out by the Civilian Conservation Corps. Reconstruction of each site was based on

The Second Lincoln-Berry Store as it appeared in the 1930s, shortly after the village of New Salem was reconstructed.

extensive research into plats, biographies, letters, and reminiscences, as well as archaeological excavations of the foundations.

Today New Salem contains 22 reconstructed buildings, as well as one original log cabin, the Onstot Cooper Shop, which had been moved to Petersburg in 1840 and returned in the 1930s. Each building is furnished with period antiques, many of which belonged to pioneer settlers of Menard County. Visiting the Second Lincoln-Berry store at the end of New Salem's main street, one can almost imagine 23-year-old Abraham Lincoln behind the counter, joking with customers as he totaled their purchases.

Customers in Lincoln and Berry's store would often play cards in front of the fireplace.

From candlesticks to farm tools to sewing notions, 1830s frontier stores carried a variety of merchandise necessary to rural life.

2. LINCOLN LOG CABIN STATE HISTORIC SITE

The Lincoln Log Cabin State Historic Site, reconstructed home of Lincoln's father and stepmother.

Visit the Lincoln Log Cabin at 402 South Lincoln Highway Road, Lerna.

Thomas Lincoln

THOMAS LINCOLN LIVED THE

last decade of his life in a small, two-room cabin in Coles County. To Abraham Lincoln this cabin represented both a way of life he tried to leave behind and family connections that he would not or could not completely sever.

In 1830 21-year-old Abraham left Indiana and moved to Illinois with 12 members of his extended family. The group included his father; stepmother Sarah (Sally) Bush Johnston Lincoln;

stepbrother John D. Johnston; stepsister Elizabeth Johnston Hanks; Elizabeth's husband (and Lincoln's cousin) Dennis Hanks; four Hanks children; stepsister Matilda Johnston Hall; Matilda's husband, Squire Hall; and the Halls' son. The family initially lived in Macon County, near Decatur, but within a year moved to Coles County. Throughout the 1830s Thomas Lincoln bought, sold, and traded parcels of land within the county, finally settling on an 80-acre tract in an area known as Goosenest Prairie. Abraham, however, was not with them. With ambitions greater than the farm life he had been raised to, he had struck out on his own in 1831, first taking a flatboat trip to New Orleans, then residing for six years in the commercial village of New Salem, and finally moving to Springfield in 1837 after being admitted to the local bar.

Thomas's life at Goosenest Prairie was a far cry from Lincoln's refined life in Springfield. No longer a young man, Thomas suffered from failing eyesight that forced him to abandon his work as a cabinetmaker and support himself through farming alone. With his son in Springfield and his stepson, John, unwilling to provide much help around the farm, Thomas lacked the necessary labor to make his farm prosperous or his home genteel.

Even after he left home, Lincoln saw to the well-being of his parents. "I desire that neither Father or Mother shall be in want of any comfort either in

Thomas Lincoln's cabin as it appeared in 1883.

Sarah Bush Johnston Lincoln

health or sickness while they live," he wrote to his stepbrother, John. To that end, Lincoln would visit his father's family when his legal business took him to Coles County. According to his niece Harriet, Lincoln never failed to bring gifts such as bolts of cloth, coffee beans, and cash.

After his father's death, Lincoln continued to look after his stepmother. Sally Lincoln had "proved a good and kind mother" to him after his own mother's death, and Lincoln often wrote to John with advice and directions on how best to care for her. Two weeks before Lincoln left for Washington, D.C., in 1861, he paid a visit to Coles County to bid farewell to the woman he called "Mother." He met her in the home of her daughter Matilda in the small town of Farmington, where Sally was staying while repairs were being done to her own cabin. "My dear boy, I always thought there was something great in you," she reportedly told him.

After Sally's death in 1869, the cabin and farm remained in her family. In 1891 Sally's grandson, John J. Hall, sold the cabin to a group of Chicago businessmen who planned to exhibit it at the World's Columbian Exposition in Chicago. The cabin was dismantled and transported to Chicago, but permission was never granted to exhibit the cabin, and the logs were lost. In 1929 the state of Illinois acquired the original 80-acre tract of the Lincoln farm from Hall's descendants. Seven years later, using photographs and archaeological evidence, the Civilian Conservation Corps re-created an exact replica of Thomas and Sarah's cabin on its original site.

Today the Lincoln Log Cabin is part of an 86-acre historic site owned and maintained by the state of Illinois. The Lincoln cabin operates as the center of a working living history farm. A visitors' center provides an introduction to 1840s farm life through exhibits and period artifacts. At the cabin, visitors may see a fire burning in the fireplace or historic trades being practiced on the grounds. The site also includes the 1840s home of upwardly mobile farmer

Stephen Sargent, whose progressive farming techniques stand in contrast to Thomas Lincoln's traditional subsistence farming. Less than a mile up the road is the Moore Home, where Abraham Lincoln said goodbye to his beloved stepmother for the last time and which is open to the public periodically for special events.

The interior of the Lincoln Log Cabin, re-created by the Civilian Conservation Corps in 1936, now interprets the lives of Lincoln's family to the public.

3. LINCOLN HOME NATIONAL HISTORIC SITE

The Lincoln Home National Historic Site in Springfield, where Lincoln lived from 1844 to 1861.

Begin your tour of the Lincoln Home at the Visitors' Center, 726 South Seventh Street, Springfield.

THE "QUAKER BROWN" HOUSE WITH GREEN SHUTTERS AT THE

corner of Eighth and Jackson Streets is the only home Abraham Lincoln ever owned. Within its clapboard walls, Lincoln grew from a young, ambitious lawyer to the president-elect of the United States; from a new husband and father of one son to a long-married father of three who had buried a child along the way.

The Lincolns bought the story-and-a-half, six-room house in 1844 for $1,200 plus the transfer of a lot worth $300. Homeownership was a huge step up from Lincoln's previous living arrangements. As a boy he shared a one-room log cabin with as many as seven other people; as a single man he

Circled numbers locate four Lincoln-related houses in Springfield.

boarded with friends; and as a young newlywed he and Mary lived in an 8-by-14-foot room in the Globe Tavern, where their first son, Robert Todd, was born in 1843, and then in a rented, three-room cottage on Fourth Street. Buying a house signaled Lincoln's arrival as a successful urban gentleman.

Three children were born to the Lincolns at Eighth and Jackson. Edward was born in 1846. A sickly child, he died of tuberculosis in 1850, just shy of his fourth birthday, and his funeral was held in the parlor. William (Willie) was born in 1850, and Thomas (Tad) was born in 1853. The surviving Lincoln boys were a boisterous lot, and on any given day they could be found playing knights, putting on a circus in the backyard, or climbing over their tolerant father.

With a thriving law practice, a burgeoning political career, and a growing family to accommodate, the Lincolns made several alterations to their home over the years. The most significant one took place in 1856, when the house was enlarged to a full two stories. Additions to the house included a dining room, so Mary could entertain company properly, and separate but

No images of the Lincolns inside their home in Springfield are known to exist, but this composite image of them in Washington, D.C., evokes the close-knit family circle that was forged in their Springfield home.

The Lincoln home as it appeared in 1860. Abraham, Tad, and Willie Lincoln are inside the fence; the boys' friend Isaac Diller is on the sidewalk below.

connecting bedrooms for the Lincolns, following middle-class fashion of the day, so Lincoln could work late or Mary could tend to the boys without disturbing her husband.

Mary's skills as a homemaker helped her husband offer a refined environment to entertain his business and political acquaintances. In May 1860 a delegation of gentlemen from the Republican convention called on Lincoln in his parlor to formally offer him the nomination as the Republican candidate for president. Later that summer, newspaper reporters from across the nation visited the home and described it in detail. "I found Mr. Lincoln living in a handsome, but not pretentious, double two-story house, having a wide hall running through the centre, with parlors on both sides, neatly, but not ostentatiously furnished," wrote a correspondent from the *New York Post*.

After Lincoln's election to the presidency, the Lincolns sold much of their furniture and arranged to rent out their house. They left for Washington, D.C., on February 11, 1861, never to return. Mary refused to live in the house after Lincoln died, believing the memories would be too painful. The house was rented by a series of tenants until 1887, when Robert Todd Lincoln donated it to the state of Illinois on the condition that it always be maintained and accessible to the public free of charge. In 1972 the house was transferred to the federal government and designated a National Historic Site.

In 1860 Frank Leslie's Illustrated Newspaper *sent an artist to sketch the Lincoln home's front parlor (pictured), rear parlor, and sitting room.*

Today the Lincoln Home is meticulously restored to its circa 1860 appearance. Some of the furnishings are original to the family, offering an intimate glimpse into Lincoln's domestic life. The boys' stereoscope on the sitting room table reflects a home where the children were loved and indulged. Mary's many decorative touches, such as French wallpaper in the bedroom, speak to the pains she took to make an attractive home for her family. Lincoln's small pigeonhole desk in the corner is a relic of the nights he spent working on legal documents and political speeches.

The Lincoln Home sits in the middle of a restored four-block neighborhood. Two nearby structures, the Dean and Arnold Houses, contain exhibits and are open to the public. Tours of the Lincoln Home begin in the visitors' center, where an introductory film provides background into the Lincolns' lives at home.

The restored front parlor in the Lincoln Home includes many items that belonged to the family.

4. VACHEL LINDSAY HOME STATE HISTORIC SITE

The Vachel Lindsay Home State Historic Site was home first to Lincoln's sister- and brother-in-law, Ann and Clark Smith, and later to famed poet Vachel Lindsay.

Visit the Vachel Lindsay Home at 603 South Fifth Street, Springfield.

IN THE 1840S AND 1850S, ABRAHAM LINCOLN WAS A

frequent visitor to his sister- and brother-in-law's two-story frame house on South Fifth Street. In the late 19th and early 20th centuries, that house was home to Vachel Lindsay, one of the most famous poets of his generation.

Constructed in the mid-1840s, the house was sold in 1853 to Clark M. Smith, whose wife, Ann, was a younger sister of Mary Lincoln.

Ann was well known in Springfield as being "quick tempered and vituperative." Mary and Ann had a thorny relationship; Mary once wrote that "poor unfortunate Ann" possessed a "miserable disposition and so false a tongue." Still, family was family, and the Todd sisters of Springfield frequently socialized with one another in each other's homes. In the winter of 1855, a family member wrote that they "dined at Mr Smiths, in company

Clark M. Smith   Ann Todd Smith

with Dr and Fanny Wallace, Mr Lincoln and Mary, Mr Edwards and Elizabeth. . . ."

Despite their differences, the Todd sisters also stuck together in difficult times. When the Smiths lost their ten-year-old son, Clark Jr., to typhoid in 1860, Mary wrote that "the family are almost inconsolable, & for the last week, I have spent the greater portion of my time, with them." Mary was likely also there for happier times. Clark and Ann reportedly hosted a going-away party for the Lincolns before they departed for Washington, D.C., in 1861.

The Smiths moved to a new home in 1864. In 1878 the house on South Fifth Street was purchased by Dr. Vachel Thomas Lindsay as a home for his wife, Catherine, and infant daughter, Olive. Nicholas Vachel Lindsay was born the next year, followed by three little girls, Isabel, Esther, and Eudora, who all died of scarlet fever within two weeks of each other in 1888. A final daughter, Joy, was born in 1889.

Vachel Lindsay at age 16.

Dr. Lindsay hoped that his son would follow him into medicine, but Vachel was destined to follow an artistic path. After completing his studies at the Art Institute of Chicago and William Merritt Chase's School of Art in New York, Lindsay spent many years traveling through the United States on foot, trading poems for food and lodging along the way as a modern troubadour before returning to his boyhood home. The publication of his poems "General William Booth Enters Heaven" in 1913 and "The Congo" in 1914 earned Lindsay national acclaim. In 1915 he was invited to perform his poetry for President Woodrow Wilson.

Abraham Lincoln's legacy had a profound impact on Lindsay when he was growing up in Springfield, and he deeply admired the 16th president. In Lindsay's 1913 poem "Lincoln," the poet wrote: "Would I might rouse the Lincoln in you all." A year later, at the start of World War I, Lindsay wrote "Abraham Lincoln Walks at Midnight," in which he imagined the great emancipator's spirit pacing the streets of Springfield, heartsick at the thought of another war.

In 1922 Lindsay moved to Spokane, Washington. There he married Elizabeth Connor and fathered two children. By 1929, suffering health and financial problems, Lindsay moved his family back to his boyhood home in Springfield. Depressed and exhausted, he took his own life on December 5, 1931, and died in the bedroom above the room in which he had been born.

Vachel's sister Olive owned the house until her death in 1957. Afterward, the Vachel Lindsay Association purchased the home and opened it to the public. The state of Illinois acquired the building in 1990 and undertook extensive renovations from 1994 until 2001, when the house reopened to the public on Vachel Lindsay's birthday, November 10.

The Lindsay home as it appeared after Vachel's 1929 return.

Today the Vachel Lindsay Home interprets the life and work of Springfield's most famous poet. Although remnants of Lincoln's era remain in the home's 19th-century layout and original wood trim, especially on the second floor, the house is interpreted to 1915, when Lindsay was at the height of his career. In addition to selections from Lindsay's poetry and artwork, its rooms are filled with several of the Lindsays' furnishings. In an upstairs bedroom, visitors can still see the Lindsay children's growth chart from the 1880s and 1890s on an unpapered section of wall. Visiting the Vachel Lindsay Home, one can sense the echo of Lincoln's long-ago presence, which inspired the young man who later lived there to create artistic and poetic masterpieces.

PART 2. LINCOLN'S FRIENDS AND COLLEAGUES

The sites in this section represent the homes of Abraham Lincoln's friends that survive and are open to the public throughout the Abraham Lincoln National Heritage Area. Five of the sites (Edwards Place, the Iles House, the Shastid House, the Fithian Home, and the Milton K. Alexander House) date to Lincoln's time and were known to have been visited by Lincoln. The other three (the Oglesby Mansion, the David Davis Mansion, and the C. H. Moore Homestead) were constructed after Lincoln's death. Nonetheless, their interpretations have strong ties to Lincoln and his legacy.

Abraham Lincoln had a unique ability to make friends. A journalist who had first met Lincoln in 1859 later recalled, "He greeted me cordially as though we had known each other for a long time. There was no strangeness about him. He knew men on the instant." Several of his acquaintances took note of the warm way in which Lincoln greeted people, as well as his simple and direct manner in conversing. His penchant for winning friends by telling apt or funny stories was legendary. Lincoln's friendships were a key reason why he was able to reach his full potential in life. Whether by encouraging him to study law, providing him a place to sleep, seeing him through bouts of depression, or supporting his political campaigns, his friends helped transform him from a poor laborer into the president of the United States.

The homes of Lincoln's friends that he was known to visit represent the wide range of his acquaintances. John Shastid was an old friend from his New Salem days who lived in a modest frame cottage in Pittsfield; Benjamin Edwards was a fellow attorney and relative by marriage who lived in a grand Italianate mansion in Springfield. Touring these homes today, a visitor gets the impression that Lincoln was a man who was able to move with ease between humble halls and lavish parlors, grateful for any hospitality that was offered to him.

The three homes that postdate Lincoln's life were all occupied by friends of his who had accumulated significant financial resources in their lifetime. Moore and Davis, both lawyers, made fortunes through land speculation (in fact, they were partners in business); Oglesby was a lawyer and career politician who later married a wealthy young widow. The mansions they built (or remodeled, in Moore's case) were meant to reflect their wealth and status.

5. EDWARDS PLACE HISTORIC HOME

![Edwards Place Historic Home]

Lincoln frequently enjoyed hospitality at Benjamin Edwards's home in the years before the Civil War.

Visit Edwards Place at the Springfield Art Association's campus: 700 North Fourth Street, Springfield.

TO MODERN EYES, BENJAMIN

Edwards and Abraham Lincoln were only very distantly related: Lincoln's wife's sister was married to Edwards's brother. Yet kinship connections mattered in antebellum Springfield. In Lincoln's view, according to his friend David Davis, "Ben was in the family." As such, Lincoln was a frequent guest in Edwards's home.

Benjamin S. Edwards

Benjamin Edwards was the aristocratic youngest son of Ninian Edwards, who had served as governor of the Illinois Territory, U.S. senator, and the third governor of Illinois.

Benjamin and his bride, Helen, settled in Springfield in 1840. Upon their arrival, they briefly stayed with his brother Ninian and Ninian's wife, Elizabeth. There they met Mary Todd, Elizabeth's younger sister and houseguest. Helen remembered: "[Mary] greeted me with such warmth of manner . . . saying she knew we would be great friends. This bond of friendship was continued to the end of her life."

Both lawyers, Edwards and Lincoln were professional colleagues in addition to being in-laws and personal friends.

Helen Dodge Edwards

They met in the courtroom on more than 400 occasions, either as co-counsel or opposing attorneys. They were also political allies until the dissolution of the Whig party in the mid-1850s. By the time Lincoln ran against Stephen A. Douglas for the U.S. Senate in 1858, however, Edwards had become a Democrat and Lincoln a Republican. On July 17, 1858, Edwards hosted a political rally for Douglas on his grounds. An estimated 5,000 people attended; among them was Lincoln, who took note of Douglas's talking points to address at his own rally at the State Capitol building later that evening.

Edwards's brick home north of downtown was built in 1833 and is now the oldest surviving house in Springfield. When the Edwards family purchased it in 1843 for $4,000, it was a story-and-a-half, six-room, Greek Revival dwelling. In 1857 they enlarged the house into a 15-room Italianate mansion to accommodate their growing family and desire to entertain.

The house was a social center of antebellum Springfield. During the high social season in late winter, the Edwardses hosted receptions for members of the Illinois legislature as well as the city's elite. In 1865 the house offered hospitality to the visitors who flocked to Springfield to attend Lincoln's funeral, some of whom slept on cots in the library. The funeral procession

The Edwards house after the 1857 remodel.

passed directly by the Edwardses' home, and they put out refreshments for the mourners as they made their way to Oak Ridge Cemetery.

The Edwardses' home was occupied as a private residence until 1909, when Helen died at age 89. Four years later, daughter Alice gave her parents' home to the newly incorporated Springfield Art Association for use as its headquarters. For many years, the parlors housed an art gallery, and classes were held in the upstairs bedrooms. By the middle of the 20th century, the Art Association's campus had expanded, and the art functions were moved out of the house into new buildings.

Today the Springfield Art Association maintains Edwards Place as a historic house museum. Completely restored to its mid-19th-century appearance, the mansion boasts reproductions of original Edwards family wallpaper in six rooms. Approximately one-third of the objects within belonged to the Edwards family, including several portraits, parlor furniture, a complete bedroom suite, silver serving pieces, and Helen Edwards's pre–Civil War music books. A selection of tableware recovered from an archaeological dig of an 1840s refuse pit are also on display.

The highlights of the mansion's collection are a sofa and a piano once owned by Mary Lincoln's sister, Elizabeth Edwards (Benjamin's sister-in-law). Both objects were in Elizabeth's parlor when Lincoln came to court Mary Todd, and both were present the night that the Lincolns were married.

The formal parlor, restored to its 1850s appearance.

6. ELIJAH ILES HOUSE

The Elijah Iles House, a place Lincoln knew well.

Visit the Elijah Iles House at 628 South Seventh Street, Springfield.

IN 1837, THE SAME YEAR THAT ABRAHAM LINCOLN RELOCATED to Springfield, Elijah Iles built himself a handsome frame dwelling on the corner of Sixth and Cook Streets. Most of the buildings that Lincoln knew when he first came to town have long since disappeared, but the Elijah Iles House remains, its oak floorboards still carrying the echo of Lincoln's footfalls from the days when he would pay social calls to its inhabitants.

Known as the "Father of Springfield," Elijah Iles arrived in the spring of 1821 and established the settlement's first store. Two years later, he and three other men bought four parcels of land and then surveyed, platted, and sold lots for the town site. Iles's land dealings eventually made him a wealthy man; his house, when first built, was considered one of the finest in Springfield.

During the Black Hawk War in 1832, Iles commanded the militia unit in which Lincoln served. Upon moving to Springfield, Lincoln represented Iles in several debt collection cases in circuit court. After Lincoln's death, Iles served as a pallbearer, accompanying the casket to its final resting place in Oak Ridge Cemetery.

Iles sold his home to merchant and banker Robert Irwin in 1841. Abraham and Mary Lincoln patronized Irwin's dry goods store in Springfield, and (in a time when merchants served as unofficial bankers) Lincoln also deposited money in Irwin's store safe, which he later withdrew with interest. When Lincoln went to Congress in the late 1840s, Irwin managed Lincoln's local financial affairs in his absence.

Elijah Iles

The Iles house in its original location at the corner of Sixth and Cook Streets, a block from the site it currently occupies.

Robert Irwin

Lincoln and Irwin were also personal friends. Lincoln was known to have joined a group of local gentlemen who regularly met at Irwin's home to play cards. One member of the group recalled Lincoln was "not so enthusiastic at the game" as the others, preferring instead the social aspects of the gathering.

Both Irwin and Lincoln shared a devotion to Whig, and later Republican, politics. When Lincoln ran for president in 1860, Irwin contributed $1,000 to Lincoln's campaign. Irwin accompanied Lincoln on his inaugural journey to Washington, D.C., in February 1861. Upon his return to Springfield, Irwin was again tasked with managing Lincoln's financial affairs and collecting his unpaid debts. Lincoln later characterized Irwin as "an old friend who has served me all my life."

Irwin died after a brief illness in March 1865, just a month before Lincoln was assassinated. His house stayed in his family's possession until 1891. Afterward, the house passed through a series of owners. At one point it was cut in half, moved to 1825 South Fifth Street, and reassembled. In 1993 the city of Springfield bought the house, and the Elijah Iles House Foundation was formed with the intention of restoring and maintaining the building. The house was moved again in 1998, this time to its current location on South Seventh Street, approximately a block away from where it was originally constructed. After seven years of restoration work, the house was opened to the public in fall 2005.

Key furnishings within the home have connections to the home's first two owners and to Lincoln. Portraits of Elijah Iles and Robert Irwin hang above the mantels of the formal parlors. Across the hall, a wardrobe in the corner belonged to Jack Armstrong, a friend of Lincoln's from his New Salem days. Legend has it that Lincoln carved the pegs within.

Today the Iles House tells the story of the Iles and Irwin families and their connections to Lincoln, and is a remarkable example of an early architectural tradition that has almost entirely vanished from Springfield.

A portrait of the home's second owner, Robert Irwin, keeps watch over the back parlor, furnished as it might have been when Lincoln came over to play cards.

7. SHASTID HOUSE

When in Pittsfield, Lincoln often called on John Greene Shastid at his home.

Visit the Shastid House at 326 Jefferson Street, Pittsfield.

WHEN ABRAHAM LINCOLN VISITED PITTSFIELD ON LEGAL

business, he often made it a point to walk three blocks from the court house square to Jefferson Street, where he would dine at the home of his old friend John Greene Shastid.

Lincoln had known Shastid since the early 1830s, when both men lived in New Salem. In 1836 Shastid moved his family to Pittsfield, the seat of Pike County, which at the time had only six houses. They initially resided in a one-story house measuring 20 feet by 30 feet. Two years later, Shastid built the more substantial frame house on Jefferson Street with his own hands.

The Shastids generally looked forward to Lincoln's company, but on one occasion, Lincoln's visit was a source of great frustration to the children. This visit made such an impression that the tale was handed down through the generations of the Shastid family.

According to the story, Shastid had returned from a hunting expedition with a dozen quail, known colloquially as "pigeons." His children were hungrily waiting for the quail to finish broiling when Lincoln let himself in the front door. The family invited Lincoln to stay for dinner. They offered him the place of honor at the head of the table and placed the platter of quail in front of him.

John Greene Shastid

After an initial burst of chatter, Lincoln fell silent, apparently preoccupied with some legal question. As he pondered, he ate. "One by one the pigeons disappeared into the vast Lincolnian reservoir," a Shastid grandchild recounted. "A gesture from grandmother kept all the rest from calling for pigeon." Still lost in thought, Lincoln reached out his fork and helped himself to the very last quail. As he began to eat, Shastid's young son Thomas began to cry and exclaimed, "Abe Lincoln, you're an old hog!" Lincoln, very full but also very contrite, apologized for his gluttony.

Lincoln kept in contact with the Shastids throughout his tenure in Illinois. In 1858 Thomas attended several of Lincoln's debates with Stephen A. Douglas. In his estimation, Douglas was the better

Lincoln once enjoyed an overly generous serving of quail at the Shastid house, much to the chagrin of his hosts.

Thomas W. Shastid

orator (Lincoln having a high voice and staccato speaking style), but Lincoln was the better reasoner. Thomas also observed a number of Lincoln's court cases. He thought Lincoln a rather average lawyer "except when he was fired by the thought of injustice or oppression," at which point he became "a veritable arch-angel of righteous advocacy."

In 1865 John Shastid was walking along the west side of the square in Pittsfield when news arrived from Washington that Lincoln had been assassinated. A young cooper's assistant raced down the street shouting, "Hooray, for Lincoln is dead!" "Who did you say is dead?" asked Shastid, who at that point was elderly and hard of hearing. "Abe Lincoln. I'm glad he is dead that old—," but the youth's next words were interrupted by Shastid's fist, which shot out and laid the young man flat on the sidewalk, unconscious.

The frame house where Lincoln gobbled up quail stayed in the Shastid family until the 1920s. It passed through two more owners until 1989, when it was donated to the Pike County Historical Society. In 2000 the house underwent a major restoration to return it to its Lincoln-era appearance. Today the Shastid House is open to the public for tours and special events. Visitors will learn about Lincoln's visits and see period furnishings, including a bed from the nearby Scanland Home that Lincoln reportedly slept in.

The room where Lincoln ate the Shastid family's dinner has been restored with period furnishings.

8. GOVERNOR RICHARD J. OGLESBY MANSION

The Governor Richard J. Oglesby Mansion preserves the legacy of the man responsible for Lincoln's famous nickname, the "Rail-Splitter."

Visit the Governor Richard J. Oglesby Mansion at 421 West William Street, Decatur.

RICHARD J. OGLESBY FIRST HEARD ABRAHAM LINCOLN SPEAK

in 1840 as a teenager attending a Whig rally in Springfield. Little could Oglesby have imagined that, 20 years later, he would have a hand in boosting Lincoln's candidacy for president of the United States. But at the 1860 Illinois Republican Convention, it was Oglesby who arranged for a 30-year-old rail split by Lincoln to be brought into the convention headquarters, thus giving birth to the legend of Lincoln the Rail-Splitter, the man of the people.

Both Lincoln and Oglesby were attorneys by trade and politicians by avocation. They first became acquainted as lawyers practicing on the Eighth Judicial Circuit in the 1840s. By the late 1850s both men were united in their devotion to the Republican Party and counted each other as political allies as well as personal friends. During the fourth Lincoln-Douglas debate in Charleston on

September 18, 1858, Oglesby was one of the guests given the honor of sharing the platform with Lincoln.

Lincoln lost his bid for the Senate in 1858, but his campaign vaulted him to national attention and opened the door for greater opportunities. In 1859 Oglesby was among the small circle of "original Lincoln men" urging Lincoln to consider running for president. In 1860 Oglesby was committed to ensuring that the Illinois Republican Convention in Decatur endorsed Lincoln as

Richard J. Oglesby

its presidential candidate. On the first day of the gathering, with Lincoln seated on the speaker's platform, Oglesby announced that there was an "old Democrat" outside who wished to present something to the convention. As the crowd shouted "receive it!" Isaac Jennings and Lincoln's cousin John Hanks entered bearing two rails. Stretched between them was a banner proclaiming "Abraham Lincoln The Rail Candidate" and identifying the rails as those split by Lincoln in 1830. The crowd went wild, and Lincoln was duly nominated. Oglesby later worked behind the scenes at the Republican National Convention in Chicago to help ensure that Lincoln captured the Republican nomination for president.

During the Civil War, Oglesby raised ten companies and served as the colonel of the 8th Volunteer Regiment, fighting at Forts Henry and Donelson. After being promoted to major general and sustaining severe injuries at Corinth, Oglesby left the front to serve as a judge advocate presiding over courts-martial in Washington. In 1864, with President Lincoln's blessing, Oglesby returned to Illinois to run for governor. He was elected by a comfortable margin and helped Illinois earn the distinction of being the first state in the Union to ratify the 13th Amendment. On April 14, 1865, Oglesby arrived in Washington, D.C., for a brief visit with Lincoln. He declined an invitation to accompany the Lincolns to the theater later that evening. On hearing that Lincoln had been shot, Oglesby rushed to Lincoln's bedside and was present when he died.

After the Civil War, Oglesby was reelected as governor in 1872 but served only six days before being appointed to the U.S. Senate by the Illinois legislature. In 1885 he was elected to a third term as Illinois governor, retiring from public life at the end of his term in 1889.

Oglesby's life and legacy are preserved at the Governor Richard J. Oglesby Mansion in Decatur. The house was built for Oglesby and his first wife, Anna, in 1859. By 1873 Anna had died, and Oglesby remarried, this time to a young, wealthy widow named Emma Gillette Keays. Needing space for their growing family, the Oglesbys hired a Chicago architect, William LeBaron Jenney (father of the skyscraper), to draw plans for a new house. This was constructed adjacent to their old house, which was used as a kitchen and servants' wing. The enlarged house, completed in 1874, boasted a library, dining room, parlor, sun porch, and kitchen on the first floor and several bedrooms on the second floor. The house was richly appointed with ornately carved wooden mantels, 11-foot ceilings, gas chandeliers, and pocket doors.

The Oglesbys sold the mansion in 1882 to James E. Berings, whose descendants occupied it for 90 years. In 1905, the 1859 wing of the house was removed and relocated. In 1972 the Macon County Conservation District purchased the mansion.

Today the Governor Oglesby Mansion has been painstakingly restored to its circa-1870s appearance. The library is almost unchanged from the Oglesbys'

In 1874 Oglesby expanded his home to accommodate his second wife, Emma Gillette Keays Oglesby, and their growing family.

The remodeled Oglesby mansion boasted elegant furnishings and appointments.

habitation and features its original chandelier, wallpaper, floor, mantel, and bookcases. Many Oglesby family artifacts are on display throughout the house, including furniture, objects pertaining to Oglesby's political career, and several examples of the Oglesbys' clothing. The house and its contents are an exceptional monument to one of Illinois's most distinguished citizens, whose inspired use of a wooden rail in 1860 helped launch Abraham Lincoln to the presidency.

Governor Oglesby's dining utensils and napkin ring are among the many family artifacts displayed throughout the house.

9. DAVID DAVIS MANSION
STATE HISTORIC SITE

The David Davis Mansion State Historic Site in Bloomington interprets the life of Lincoln's close friend and campaign manager, David Davis.

Visit the David Davis Mansion at 1000 East Monroe Avenue, Bloomington.

IN MANY WAYS, DAVID DAVIS AND ABRAHAM LINCOLN WERE

very different men. Davis was large and round, while Lincoln was tall and thin; Davis was a college graduate, while Lincoln had a scant year of formal schooling; Davis was wealthy and aristocratic in his tastes, while Lincoln was humble and frugal. Yet, bound by common interests in the law and politics, the two men forged a lasting bond.

Davis was born in Cecil County, Maryland, and educated at Kenyon College in Ohio and New Haven Law School in Connecticut. For two years after graduation, he studied law with a private attorney in Lenox, Massachusetts, then struck out for Illinois in 1835. After briefly settling in Pekin, he moved

to Bloomington to practice law in
1836. Two years later, he married Sarah
Walker, whom he had courted while
working in Lenox.

Davis first met Lincoln in 1836
when the latter was serving in the state
legislature. Their paths crossed often in
the subsequent decade during political campaigns in support of Whig
candidates. "Lincoln is the best stump
speaker in the State," Davis wrote in
1844. "He shows the want of early
education but he has great powers as a
speaker."

David Davis

As attorneys, Lincoln and Davis
often met each other on the circuit. Davis's election as circuit judge in 1848
meant that, for many years afterward, they were together for 10 to 12 weeks
each spring and fall as they traveled almost 500 miles through the counties
of the circuit. After court had adjourned, Davis and the lawyers would often
retire to a local inn and swap stories with the courtroom attendees and members of the community.

Davis supported Lincoln's rise to political prominence. In 1860 he was one
of the first men to encourage Lincoln to run for president. At the Republican
National Convention in Chicago, Davis oversaw the behind-the-scenes wheel-
ing and dealing required to amass enough delegate votes to secure Lincoln's
nomination. During the general election, Davis managed Lincoln's campaign
and helped steer him to victory. Contemporaries said that Lincoln would not
have been nominated were it not for the effort and acumen of Davis.

Davis expected to be rewarded with a federal appointment right away, but
it was more than a year and a half before Lincoln nominated him to a vacancy
on the U.S. Supreme Court. The friendship between the two men cooled a
bit during this interval: Lincoln was annoyed at Davis's hunger for office, and
Davis resented what he perceived to be Lincoln's ingratitude for all his help.

Still, Davis continued to be an important figure in Lincoln's life, and in
the lives of his family. When Lincoln was assassinated in 1865, Robert Lincoln sent an urgent telegram requesting Davis come to Washington, D.C., at
once to take charge of his father's financial affairs. Davis thereafter served as

When Lincoln knew him, David Davis lived in this two-story frame house on the east side of Bloomington.

the legal guardian for Lincoln's young son Tad as well as the administrator of Lincoln's estate.

The Davises' home site was named "Clover Lawn." In 1870 David and Sarah hired Alfred Piquenard, the French architect who designed the current Illinois state capitol, to design a new residence on the location of the two-story frame house in which they had lived for 30 years. Their grand new home was completed in 1872. The three-story, yellow-brick mansion had 36 rooms and modern conveniences such as gas lighting, indoor plumbing, and a coal-burning furnace.

Davis left the Supreme Court in 1877 when he was elected to the U.S. Senate. He retired to Clover Lawn in 1883 and died three years later. Clover Lawn remained in the Davis family until 1959, when David Davis IV and his nieces deeded the estate to the state of Illinois. The gift included the entire contents of the mansion, spanning five generations of the Davis family's possessions, as well as the Davis family papers. This manuscript collection includes the newsy letters Davis wrote to Sarah while he was a circuit-riding judge, which provide valuable information about life and Lincoln on the circuit, as well as 20 documents in Lincoln's hand. In 1987 the mansion underwent a full-scale restoration.

Today, the David Davis Mansion is operated by the state of Illinois. Visitors will see a perfectly preserved example of gilded-age living, as almost everything in the mansion is original to the Davis family. Although the mansion was built after Lincoln's death, visitors will learn about the remarkable friendship between Davis and Lincoln and the influence that friendship had on Lincoln's election to the presidency. Noteworthy is the barn to the rear of the mansion, which dates to the 1850s, where Lincoln reportedly stabled his horse.

Clover Lawn as it appeared in the 19th century.

The Davis Mansion has been restored to its 1870s appearance.

10. C. H. MOORE HOMESTEAD

Clifton H. Moore's homestead is owned and operated by the DeWitt County Museum.

Visit the C. H. Moore Homestead at 219 East Woodlawn Street, Clinton.

TWICE A YEAR, FOR MORE THAN 20 YEARS, ABRAHAM

Lincoln's legal work on the Eighth Judicial Circuit took him to Clinton, the DeWitt County seat. Between 1839 and 1860, Lincoln spent more than 100 evenings in Clinton, where he formed friendships with local political allies and professional acquaintances.

One friend and ally was Clifton H. Moore. A native of Ohio, Moore came to Illinois in 1839 at the age of 22. Two years later, having passed the bar in Pekin, he moved to Clinton and became the town's first resident attorney. By the mid-1850s, Lincoln and Moore were both on retainer as attorneys for the Illinois Central Railroad and often worked together on railroad cases. From 1856 to 1858 Moore even shared his law office with Lincoln when Lincoln was in Clinton for court.

The two men shared interests beyond the law. Both were avid readers. They were also staunch Republicans. On September 2, 1858, during Lincoln's campaign for the Senate, Moore helped to organize a Republican barbeque in

Clinton with Lincoln as the featured speaker. Despite a heavy rain, more than 10,000 people attended the mass meeting.

After delivering his speech in Clinton, Lincoln spent the night in Moore's large brick home on the outskirts of town. Moore occupied this residence until 1880, when he purchased a spacious frame house from his brother-in-law, John Bishop. Although Lincoln never visited this second home, it stands as a window into the world of a prosperous central Illinois attorney and thus provides a glimpse of the life Lincoln might have led had he survived his presidency.

Clifton H. Moore

By the 1880s Moore had become an extremely wealthy man. He had bought land over several decades, eventually acquiring 25,000 acres. Much of the land had been purchased in partnership with David Davis at public auction when its owners defaulted on paying real estate taxes. Moore's net worth

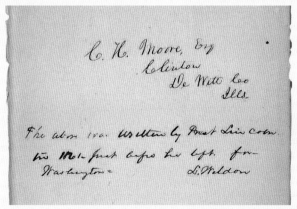

Lincoln borrowed Types of Mankind *from Moore's extensive library, then wrote Moore's name on the flyleaf, presumably to remind himself from whom he had borrowed it.*

was estimated to be more than a million dollars, which translates to roughly $28 million today.

When Moore moved into his new home in 1880, he made improvements that reflected his status and affluence. He installed running water and constructed a new kitchen and servants' quarters. The most notable upgrade was the 1887 addition of a two-story library wing, built to house Moore's collection of more than 7,000 volumes.

Moore and his wife Minerva were the last owner-occupants of the mansion. He died in 1901; she in 1907. For more than half a century, the Moore home was rented out. The DeWitt County Museum acquired the mansion in 1967, when it was on the verge of being demolished.

Today the home has been restored to its late 19th-century appearance. Many Moore family furnishings, including the library table, chairs, and bookcases in the library and an inlaid table with matching pier mirror in the front parlor, are on display. The basement showcases exhibits on local history, including a collection of military memorabilia and a simulated log cabin.

One of the most remarkable features of the homestead is the two-story library.

Abraham Lincoln is said to have used this desk, displayed in the homestead's basement, which was owned by early Clinton pioneer John McGraw.

11. FITHIAN HOME

The Dr. William Fithian Home in Danville, where Lincoln spent the night on September 21, 1858.

Visit the Fithian Home at the Vermilion County Museum, 116 North Gilbert Street, Danville.

FROM 1841 TO 1859, LINCOLN'S

legal work usually brought him to Danville, the seat of Vermilion County, every spring and fall. While there, he often visited his friend and supporter Dr. William Fithian at his spacious brick mansion on the outskirts of town.

Lincoln and Fithian had been sworn in as Whig representatives to the Illinois state legislature on the same day in 1834. In 1838 Fithian was elected to the first of two terms in the Illinois Senate; Lincoln continued to serve in the Illinois House of

Dr. William Fithian

Representatives until 1842. Fithian's support of Lincoln was a significant factor in Lincoln's rise in the Illinois legislature as well as in the expansion of his law practice in Vermilion County.

Lincoln represented Fithian in court six times. In one case, Fithian sued George W. Casseday for libel after he claimed that Fithian abandoned his wife when she died and left her to be buried by others. Fithian sought a massive $25,000 in damages; the jury awarded him $547.90, an amount significant enough to restore Fithian's reputation.

Fithian was widowed three times before marrying Josephine Black in 1850. Shortly after their marriage, Fithian began construction on a large brick home for his new family, which

Josephine Black Fithian, William Fithian's fourth wife.

included his bride, two sons, and four stepchildren. Fithian had built a large fortune from the mercantile activities, banking, politics, and land speculation he engaged in on the side of his medical practice. The house he built for his family, completed in 1855, was one of the town's most elite dwellings.

On September 21, 1858, Lincoln arrived in Danville by train to attend a Republican rally the next afternoon as part of his campaign for a seat in the U.S. Senate. A crowd met him at the depot and accompanied him the half mile to Fithian's home, where Lincoln was staying overnight. Once there, the crowd began calling for Lincoln to make a speech. The local newspaper recorded that "Lincoln appeared on the balcony and made a few remarks which were frequently interrupted by the most vociferous cheering you ever heard. . . . He thanked them for the kind reception and retired." Legend has it that he delivered his remarks in his stockings because his feet were too swollen from traveling to put on his boots again.

Today the Vermilion County Museum owns and interprets the home. On the second story visitors will see the bedroom where Lincoln stayed,

Lincoln spoke from this balcony when he visited the Fithian house in 1858.

boasting the pine floors on which he walked, the bed in which he slept, and the balcony from which he spoke. Downstairs, a recreation of Fithian's office includes his hat, scarf, rocking chair, and saddlebags, as well as a sofa Lincoln was known to sit on, once owned by Danville attorney Oliver L. Davis.

Next door to the Fithian Home, the Vermilion County Museum exhibits a replica of the law office Lincoln shared with Ward Hill Lamon when he was in Danville, including the desk at which he used to work. This desk descended through the family of Hiram Beckwith, who had studied law with Lincoln and Lamon and eventually took over Lamon's office.

The bedroom in which Lincoln stayed has been restored to its 1850s appearance. The bed is original to the home.

12. MILTON K. ALEXANDER HOUSE

Lincoln was a frequent guest at Milton K. Alexander's home in Paris.

The Milton K. Alexander House is owned by the Paris Bicentennial Art Center. Visit it at 132 South Central Avenue, Paris.

FROM 1845 TO 1853, THE EIGHTH

Judicial Circuit included Edgar County, on the eastern edge of the state, bordering Indiana. Although Paris, its county seat, was more than 100 miles from his home in Springfield, Abraham Lincoln nevertheless had many friends and acquaintances there. One of them was Milton K. Alexander.

Born in Georgia in 1796, Alexander served under General Andrew Jackson during the War of 1812. In 1823 he, his wife Mary, and their two small children settled

Milton K. Alexander

in Paris, where he opened the county's first store. Alexander's fortunes and family both flourished; he became a prosperous merchant and land speculator and fathered six more children.

In 1828 Alexander built the town's first brick house, a two-story, Federal-style home with two rooms downstairs and two rooms upstairs. In 1834, this house was enlarged by a brick addition to the rear which nearly doubled its size.

Lincoln and Alexander likely met during their service in the Black Hawk War. Later, when Lincoln's law practice took him to Edgar County, he often visited Alexander at his home. Milton's daughter Lucy later said that according to her family, the first time she met Lincoln, "I celebrated the occasion by taking my first steps in his presence." On one memorable occasion, Lincoln and Stephen A. Douglas visited the Alexander house together in 1840; Lincoln came to pay a social call and Douglas came to court Milton's daughter

The Alexander home as it appeared in 1890 after two significant additions.

Jane. The young lady, however, preferred the attentions of another suitor and escaped out a back window when she saw Douglas coming. The refined social setting of the Alexander home attracted Lincoln and other lawyers of the Eighth Judicial Circuit when court met in Edgar County. Weakened by a disease he caught during the War of 1812, Alexander was considered an invalid for the last ten years of his life and preferred to receive people at home rather than meet them out in society.

Lincoln and Alexander crossed paths in the courtroom on seven occasions. In five cases, Lincoln represented the party opposing Alexander (once in front of the Illinois Supreme Court). Twice Alexander hired Lincoln; the second time, Lincoln neglected to attend to Alexander's case at the spring term of court and was forced to write to Alexander telling him he would tend to it in the fall. The final judgment was rendered two months before Alexander died in 1856.

The Alexander home remained in the family until the twentieth century. In the 1890s the house was remodeled to feature a single-story, open front porch

Lincoln called on Milton Alexander when attending court in Edgar County.

and a crenellated, two-story bay window to the rear. In 1918 Milton Alexander's son sold the home to the Link family, who retained it until 1980.

Today the home serves as the headquarters of the Paris Bicentennial Art Center and Museum. The parlors where Lincoln once came to call now host rotating art exhibits, and the bedroom to which Alexander retired now houses art classroom space. While the interior of the house has evolved to accommodate its new mission, the Art Center and Museum remains committed to preserving and sharing its connection to Lincoln. Staff are eager to walk visitors through the house and help them imagine it as Lincoln must have seen it.

The Art Center and Museum maintains a "Lincoln corner" in its front office.

PART 3. LINCOLN'S TIMES AND LEGACY

The ten sites profiled in this section illuminate the times in which Lincoln lived or the legacy he left behind. Only two sites—the William Watson Hotel and the Bryant Cottage State Historic Site—have strong evidence that Lincoln was ever there. A handful of others are places Lincoln might have visited, such as the Broadwell Inn, the Duncan Mansion, and the John Wood Mansion, while the rest are places Lincoln likely never saw. Yet all of these sites provide insight into Lincoln's world or the way his legacy shaped the world after his death.

Between his legal work and his time devoted to politics, Lincoln spent an extraordinary amount of time on the road in Illinois. The Broadwell Inn and the William Watson Hotel illustrate the types of accommodations Lincoln had access to while traveling. The Broadwell Inn is typical of the roadside taverns in which Lincoln took meals or spent the night on the lonely roads between county seats on the circuit, and the William Watson Hotel represents the more commodious accommodations offered by town hotels.

The Joseph Duncan Mansion and the John Wood Mansion were the residences of two men who served as governor of Illinois. Because Duncan and Wood both worked from their homes, each house served as the official Illinois executive residence during its occupant's time in office. While it is unknown whether Lincoln ever visited either house, it is certain that Duncan and Wood both had a significant impact on the Illinois antebellum political landscape and the men (like Lincoln) who were part of it.

The Bryant Cottage State Historic Site and the Reddick Mansion are two of the most important sites associated with the Lincoln-Douglas debates in Illinois. Lincoln and Douglas reportedly hammered out the details of their debates at the Bryant Cottage, and the Reddick Mansion is the only surviving structure on Ottawa's town square that was visible to Lincoln as he participated in the first debate.

The Richard Eells and Trobaugh-Good Houses and the Joseph Smith Homestead and Mansion House site all shed light on vital issues of Lincoln's day. Dr. Eells was a Quincy abolitionist who tried to help a runaway slave escape to freedom; at his house, visitors get an in-depth view of the thorny issues of slavery and abolition in Illinois. The Trobaugh-Good house was a typical antebellum farmer's residence, and Joseph Trobaugh was a typical Illinois farmer, someone who had come west and purchased land in search of a better life. Although Lincoln likely did not know Trobaugh personally, his world (and legal clientele) was filled with men just like Trobaugh. The Joseph Smith Homestead and Mansion House in Nauvoo provides a fascinating glimpse into the history of Latter-day Saints, as well as the trials and triumphs of its leader, Joseph Smith. While it is unknown whether Lincoln and Smith ever met, Lincoln was nevertheless aware of Smith's exploits, which filled Springfield's daily papers in the early 1840s.

Finally, the Carl Sandburg State Historic Site was not built in Lincoln's lifetime, but Lincoln's legacy was still very much alive in Galesburg. Born there in 1878, the son of Swedish immigrants, Carl Sandburg grew up steeped in stories of Lincoln. As an adult, he found his literary voice and immortalized Lincoln in a groundbreaking set of biographies that are still cherished today.

By touring these sites, visitors have the chance to immerse themselves in Lincoln's Illinois and explore the conditions, people, and issues that filled Lincoln's thoughts and shaped his world.

13. GOVERNOR JOSEPH DUNCAN MANSION

The Governor Joseph Duncan Mansion served as the official executive residence in the 1830s.

Visit the Governor Duncan Mansion at 4 Duncan Place, Jacksonville.

THE GOVERNOR JOSEPH DUNCAN MANSION IN JACKSONVILLE IS

one of two Illinois executive residences still standing outside of Springfield. Duncan occupied this home from 1834 until his death in 1844. The building served as the governor's mansion during his single term in office, from 1834 to 1838.

Duncan was Illinois's only Whig governor. The Whig party was in the minority in 1830s Illinois, a time and place dominated by supporters of Andrew Jackson and the Democratic Party. Initially elected to the U.S. House of Representatives as a Jacksonian Democrat, Duncan broke with the Democratic Party in 1834. Word of this split, however, did not reach Illinois in time to prevent Duncan from being elected governor of Illinois in absentia on the Democratic ticket that year. Detained in Washington, D.C., by a family illness after the close of the congressional session, Duncan arrived in Illinois in August 1834 to learn that he had defeated three rival Democrats to become the sixth governor of Illinois.

He took office the same year that twenty-five-year-old Abraham Lincoln first took his seat as a member of the Illinois House of Representatives. Lincoln, also a Whig, personally wrote several letters to Duncan requesting patronage appointments for various worthy acquaintances.

Both politics and the law took Lincoln to Jacksonville frequently. Although there is no direct evidence, it is possible that Lincoln was a guest in Duncan's Jacksonville home. In addition to being fellow Whigs who were active in state government, Lincoln and Duncan shared a mutual acquaintance in Dr. John Todd. A good friend to the Duncan family, Todd was Mary Lincoln's uncle and the de facto patriarch of the Springfield Todds.

Joseph Duncan

Certainly the Duncan mansion was a social center of early Jacksonville. Built in 1834, the three-story, 17-room house was one of the grandest homes in town. Within the home's high-ceilinged rooms, political luminaries such as John J. Hardin, Stephen A. Douglas, and Daniel Webster were entertained in a setting unusually genteel for an early prairie town. Duncan's wife, Elizabeth, had been a Washington, D.C., socialite when she captured the eye of then-congressman Duncan. Moving west to Illinois, Elizabeth brought with her several fine pieces of furniture, silver, and glassware that had belonged to her parents. She also brought her mahogany square grand piano, which lent a touch of culture and refinement to her frontier surroundings.

Only four and a half feet tall, Elizabeth was a pint-sized force of nature. She managed a large household that included her children, servants, and a never-ending stream of houseguests, yet still found time to devote to civic interests.

Joseph Duncan died at home at age 49 in 1844 after a brief illness. The house remained in the Duncan family until 1920, when it was given to the Rev. James Caldwell Chapter of the Daughters of the American Revolution for use as their headquarters. This organization owns and operates the house today. The interior has been restored to interpret the Duncans' residence in the 1830s and 1840s. Many family furnishings are on display, including several pieces of furniture by local cabinetmaker James S. Anderson, Elizabeth's piano, and paintings by the Duncans' daughter Julia. Visiting this mansion is an opportunity to step into the world of early Illinois's social and political elite: the world that Lincoln, as a young congressman, aspired to enter.

The Duncan Mansion as it appeared in the 19th century, when it was known as Elm Grove.

Today Elizabeth Duncan's portrait hangs over the mantel where, according to tradition, her six-foot-tall husband used to place her when she annoyed him. She would be stranded here until a servant could be summoned to help her down.

The Duncan mansion is furnished with several pieces of family furniture, including the governor's bed.

14. BROADWELL INN

The Broadwell Inn provided food and shelter for travelers from 1824 to 1847.

Visit the Broadwell Inn at 125 County Highway 9C, Pleasant Plains.

WHILE CRISSCROSSING CENTRAL ILLINOIS ON THE EIGHTH

Judicial Circuit, Abraham Lincoln became intimately familiar with the taverns that dotted the rural landscape between towns and offered food and lodging to weary travelers. One of the oldest and best-preserved examples of an early 19th-century tavern is the Broadwell Inn, part of the Clayville Historic Site just outside the village of Pleasant Plains.

The Broadwell family arrived on the land now occupied by the Broadwell Inn in December 1819 from Ohio. They liked the area and became squatters on the land until the first federal land sales in 1824, when patriarch Moses bought nearly 3,000 acres. That same year, they constructed an inn and a dwelling house nearby from brick fired on-site.

These brick structures stood out on the sparsely settled countryside. In 1825 the legendary Methodist circuit preacher Peter Cartwright tried to entice people to settle in Sangamon County by describing the Broadwells' buildings: "Brick houses don't grow on trees in this country; but, there are two brick houses within a mile of my log cabin. One was built for a public inn. . . . This building is the wonder of the Sangamo Country." After Moses's death in 1827, his family continued to operate the inn for the next 20 years.

When it was in use, the inn was known as the Clayville Inn after the famous statesman, Henry Clay. Located on the road between Springfield and Beardstown, it offered meals and overnight accommodations to stagecoach travelers, itinerant lawyers and preachers, cattle drovers, and freight carriers. The going rate for services was 25 cents for meals, 12½ cents for lodging, and 12½ cents for stabling. In addition, the inn served as a community gathering place: locals would drop in for an evening to drink and play cards, and dances were held in the upstairs ballroom.

No surviving records document Abraham Lincoln's relationship with the Broadwells' tavern. It is unlikely that he spent the night there, as it was only half a day's journey from Springfield. However, Lincoln probably stopped there for meals on his way to and from Virginia and Beardstown, where he occasionally practiced law.

After John Broadwell sold the Clayville Inn in 1847, it passed through a series of owners. By the middle of the 20th century, it was being used as a

The Broadwell family sold the inn in 1847. By the early 20th century, it was being used as housing for local tenant farmers, shown here in 1916.

By the early 2000s, nature had largely reclaimed the historic inn.

tenant house for farmers. In 1961 the property was purchased by a Springfield physician, Dr. Emmet Pearson, who restored the site and brought in additional 19th-century buildings to make a historic village. In 1972 Pearson donated the site to Sangamon State University, which operated it as the Clayville Rural Life Center for the next 20 years. After being sold to private hands in the 1990s, the site was abandoned and grew increasingly more dilapidated.

The Pleasant Plains Historical Society purchased the inn in 2010. The property includes two 19th-century log cabins, two barns, and a blacksmith shop. The Broadwell Inn has been restored and is interpreted to the public as an early 19th-century stagecoach stop and tavern. Inside, the inn boasts its original black walnut trim and mantels as well as an intact kitchen hearth and bake oven. It is furnished with period antiques, including a bed that once belonged to Peter Cartwright. Stepping into the Broadwell Inn, visitors can imagine Lincoln seated at the dining table in the main hall or in front of the fire in the gentleman's parlor, sharing stories with fellow lawyers and local farmers over a meal before saddling up his horse and continuing on his journey.

Cooking at the inn was done over an open fireplace with attached bake oven. Tavern food was often simple, hearty fare such as beef or pork, potatoes, eggs, bread, and stew.

It was common practice for 19th-century travelers to share beds like these with strangers in public inns.

15. CARL SANDBURG STATE HISTORIC SITE

The Carl Sandburg State Historic Site, where the poet and writer was born and spent the first year and a half of his life.

Visit the Carl Sandburg State Historic Site at 313 East Third Street, Galesburg.

CARL SANDBURG WAS BORN ON JANUARY 6, 1878, IN THIS

tiny cottage on Third Street in Galesburg. From his humble birth as the child of working-class Swedish immigrants, Sandburg went on to achieve literary acclaim as a Pulitzer Prize–winning writer. Among his most lasting achievements is a six-volume biography of Abraham Lincoln that has been hailed as the "best-selling, most widely read, most influential book about Lincoln" ever written.

Sandburg grew up steeped in Lincoln lore. The Galesburg of his childhood was only a few decades removed from the time when Lincoln had visited the town personally. Sandburg heard stories of Lincoln firsthand from people who had known him. He often walked in the shadow of Old Main at Knox College, the site of Lincoln's fifth debate with Stephen A. Douglas in the 1858 contest for U.S. senator. These early experiences sparked an interest in Lincoln that would stay with Sandburg throughout his life.

Nothing in Sandburg's child-hood suggested that he was destined for greatness. His father, August Sandburg, worked six days a week as a laborer for the railroad to support his family of seven children, and money was always tight in their household. The house into which Sandburg was born was a modest work-ingman's cottage of only three rooms. When he was a year and a half old, his family moved to another house in Galesburg.

Carl Sandburg

Carl Sandburg's birthplace as it appeared in the 1890s, several years after the Sandburg family moved to a new home.

Sandburg quit school after the eighth grade and took a series of odd jobs, including delivering milk, selling stereoscopes, and writing for newspapers.

Sandburg's career as a poet was launched in 1914 with the publication of six of his poems in *Poetry: A Magazine of Verse*. His first volume of poetry, *Chicago Stories*, appeared two years later and was followed by *Cornhuskers*, which was awarded the Pulitzer Prize in 1919. Sandburg became known as the poet of the common man, celebrating the voice and spirit of the American people.

Perhaps it was only natural that Sandburg was drawn to Lincoln, the quintessential American hero. With an affinity born of a childhood spent on the same prairie landscape that Lincoln himself used to walk, Sandburg began work on a biography of Lincoln in the early 1920s. Published in 1926,

Remembrance Rock, under which the ashes of Sandburg and his wife, Lilian, are buried, was named for his only novel and bears an inscription from that book: "for it could be a place to come and remember."

Abraham Lincoln: The Prairie Years was written in a style that displayed his literary roots, filled with poetic and often sentimental turns of phrase. Thirteen years later, Sandburg published a four-volume culmination of his research on Lincoln. *Abraham Lincoln: The War Years* won the Pulitzer Prize for history in 1940.

Visitors to the Carl Sandburg State Historic Site will see the three-room cottage where the famous poet entered the world: the parlor where Sandburg's father, August, read from the Bible; the bedroom where he was born on a corn-husk mattress; and the kitchen where Sandburg's mother, Clara, cooked the family's meals. Behind the cottage is a garden where the ashes of Sandburg and his wife lay buried under a granite boulder known as Remembrance Rock. Next door to the cottage, a visitors' center contains an excellent exhibit on the poet's life and works. Like Lincoln, Sandburg rose from humble beginnings to national acclaim. The tiny cottage at the Carl Sandburg State Historic Site stands as a testament to the American spirit that propelled a poor Kentucky boy to the White House and the poor Galesburg boy who admired him to the status of national literary icon.

Next door to the home site, a visitors' center contains an exhibit about Sandburg that includes many artifacts the poet and his family owned.

16. JOSEPH SMITH HOMESTEAD AND MANSION HOUSE

The Joseph Smith Mansion House, built in 1843.

Visit the Joseph Smith Homestead and Mansion House at 865 Water Street, Nauvoo.

FROM 1839 TO 1844, THE ORBITS OF ABRAHAM LINCOLN AND

Joseph Smith's lives passed closely to one another on numerous occasions. While it is uncertain whether these two men ever met, they knew some of the same people and, on more than one occasion, were in the same place at the same time. Lincoln certainly knew of Smith and his religious followers, whose exploits regularly were reported on in the Springfield papers, and Smith may have known of Lincoln through Lincoln's work in the state legislature.

Smith was born in Vermont in 1805 and raised on a farm in western New York. In 1823 Smith claimed to have been visited by an angel who revealed the location of a book of golden plates written in an unknown language. Later Smith translated and transcribed these plates, which he published in 1830 as the *Book of Mormon*. This text became the foundation of a new religion of which Smith was the Prophet. His followers eventually called themselves the Latter-day Saints (commonly known as "Mormons").

Throughout the 1830s the Saints established colonies both in Kirtland, Ohio, and in western Missouri. Smith resided in Ohio until early 1838, when internal divisions and financial difficulties caused the Kirtland Mormon community to founder. Smith and thousands of Saints fled to Missouri, only to face hostility from non-Mormons, who saw the newcomers as a political and religious threat. When tensions boiled over into violent skirmishes between Mormons and non-Mormons in the summer of 1838, Missouri governor Lilburn Boggs issued an executive order stating that Mormons must be exterminated or driven from the state.

Joseph Smith

As a result, Smith and more than 10,000 of his followers sought refuge in Illinois, first in Quincy, then on land Smith purchased in the small town of Commerce in Hancock County on the Mississippi River. Smith rechristened this town "Nauvoo" (Hebrew for "beautiful"), and used his political connections to obtain a liberal city charter from the Illinois state legislature. Abraham Lincoln was one of the Illinois state representatives who voted in favor of the Nauvoo city charter.

On arriving in Nauvoo in 1839, Smith and his wife and children moved into a two-story log house near the river. The house served as the church's headquarters in addition to being the family's home.

In 1842 an unknown assailant shot Governor Boggs three times in the head. Boggs, who survived the attack, suspected Smith and the Saints were behind the assassination attempt and ordered that Smith be extradited to Missouri to stand trial for attempted murder. Fearing that he would be killed if he returned to Missouri, Smith went into hiding, often evading Missouri law officials by disappearing through a trapdoor in the keeping room.

After seven months of being pursued, Smith grew tired of hiding and allowed himself to be arrested and taken to Springfield for a habeas corpus hearing, which his legal advisers were confident would quash or defeat Missouri's extradition writ. The hearing took place in early January 1843, before Judge Nathanial Pope in a courtroom packed with spectators. Among them were several women, including newlywed Mary Lincoln, seated on the judge's platform for lack of space. It is unknown whether Lincoln was there

Smith and his family lived in the right side of this two-story house from 1839 to 1843. The frame addition on the left was built in the 1850s.

The "keeping room" in the rear of the house was the largest meeting space in Nauvoo at the time. It was usually filled with visitors and church officials.

to witness the proceedings; if not, he surely heard about it afterward from his wife. As anticipated, Judge Pope ruled in Smith's favor.

Smith then returned to Nauvoo and supervised construction of a much larger house across the street from the homestead. He and his family took up residence there in August 1843. This house, known as the Mansion House, was built with an adjacent hotel wing to accommodate the Prophet's many out-of-town guests. Initially, the Smiths acted as proprietors of the hotel and occupied the front bedrooms of the main house. Finding themselves too busy to be innkeepers, they soon rented the mansion to a new proprietor but reserved the right to occupy three back bedrooms.

For the next several months, tensions mounted between Mormons and their non-Mormon neighbors in western Illinois. In June 1844 Smith and his brother Hyrum were arrested on grounds of inciting a riot and placed in the Carthage jail. On June 27 an armed mob stormed the jail and shot Hyrum, killing him instantly. Smith was shot multiple times as he tried to escape through a window and died shortly after hitting the ground. His body and that of his brother were placed on view to mourners in the Mansion House in Nauvoo. Back in Springfield, Lincoln likely read all the details of the assassination in a lengthy article published in the *Illinois State Weekly Journal* on July 11.

Today the Joseph Smith Homestead and Mansion House are owned and interpreted by the Community of Christ Church. Inside the homestead, visitors can walk the same floors that Smith walked as he received divine revelations. A walking stick belonging to Emma Smith and a table belonging to the Smith family are also on view. In the Mansion House, visitors can see the large rooms initially occupied by the Smith family as well as the smaller rooms into which they later moved. The hotel wing of the mansion house is no longer extant, though the foundation remains visible in the yard. Smith, his wife Emma, and his brother Hyrum are interred in a small family cemetery on the property.

A front bedroom of the Mansion House, with a quilt made by Smith's wife Emma draped over the foot of the bedstead.

17. DR. RICHARD EELLS HOUSE

The home of Dr. Richard Eells, a noted abolitionist.

Visit the Dr. Richard Eells House at 415 Jersey Street, Quincy.

THE CITIZENS OF ABRAHAM LINCOLN'S ILLINOIS HELD MANY

different views on the contentious issue of slavery. Some were sympathetic to the institution. Some believed that slaves should be freed and colonized in Africa. Some, like Lincoln, wanted to limit the territorial spread of the institution, believing it would eventually die out on its own. Some believed in gradual, compensated emancipation. And some, like Dr. Richard Eells of Quincy, were more radical opponents of slavery who favored its immediate abolition and actively worked to help enslaved people escape to freedom.

In antebellum Illinois, aiding escaped slaves was a crime punishable by steep fines or imprisonment. Despite these risks, Eells is credited with assisting hundreds of slaves to flee their bondage. Born in Connecticut in 1800, he likely absorbed his abolitionist sentiments in the antislavery culture of New England. As a young man he obtained a medical degree from Yale University. In 1835 Eells and his wife, Jane, moved to Quincy and built an imposing brick

Dr. Richard Eells's house, built in 1835, as it appeared in the 19th century.

dwelling on Jersey Street. Eells soon became active in the local abolitionist movement, and in 1839 he was elected president of the Adams County Anti-Slavery Society.

On August 21, 1842, Eells heard knocking at his back door. He opened it to find an escaped slave named Charley, his clothes still drenched from swimming across the Mississippi River. Charley had run away from his master in Monticello, Missouri, and was looking for help. Knowing that his house was not a safe place to harbor runaways, Eells ushered Charley into his carriage and attempted to drive him to Quincy's Mission

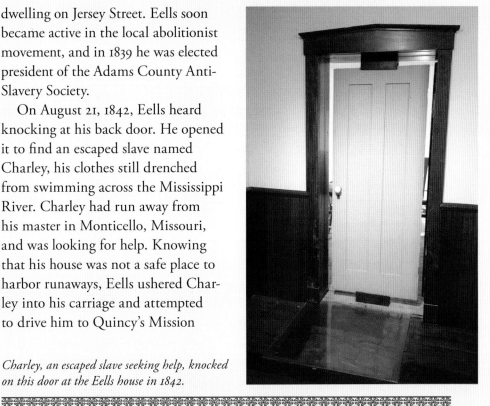

Charley, an escaped slave seeking help, knocked on this door at the Eells house in 1842.

The streets of Quincy as they appeared when Dr. Eells tried to drive Charley to safety.

Institute. On the way, they were pursued by slave catchers. Charley jumped out of the carriage and tried to flee on foot but was caught and sent back to Missouri.

Two days later, Eells was arrested and charged under Illinois law with "harboring, secreting, and assisting" a fugitive slave. He was released on bail and tried the following April when the Adams County Court met in Quincy. Judge Stephen A. Douglas heard Eells's case, found him guilty, and fined him $400. The following year the case was appealed to the Illinois Supreme Court, where the lower court's ruling was upheld.

In 1852 a group of abolitionists appealed Eells's case to the United States Supreme Court, hoping to strike a blow against slavery at the national level. Eells had died in 1846, and executors of his estate were represented before the Supreme Court by Salmon P. Chase of Ohio and William Seward of New York. (Both would run against Lincoln for the Republican nomination in 1860 and later held positions in Lincoln's cabinet.) Nevertheless, the U.S. Supreme Court upheld the state court's guilty verdict. In 2014 Eells was posthumously pardoned by Illinois governor Pat Quinn.

Today the Eells House has been designated an official National Underground Railroad Network to Freedom site by the National Park Service. It is owned by the city of Quincy and operated by the Friends of Dr. Richard Eells House. That organization has done extensive work on the house to stabilize the structure and restore the interior to its 1840s appearance. "Windows" into the walls allow visitors to glimpse original brickwork, hand-split lathe, and plaster, offering a fascinating peek into how the house evolved under Eells's ownership in the 1830s and 1840s. A number of Eells family belongings are on display in the house, as are historic documents and artifacts that provide context for the complex story of slavery and abolition in antebellum Illinois.

Fragments of glass and pottery the Eells family recovered during an archaeological excavation of the grounds are showcased on the wall of the dining room.

18. JOHN WOOD MANSION

Between 1835 and 1838, German immigrants built the home of Governor John Wood.

Visit the John Wood Mansion at 425 South 12th Street, Quincy.

DURING THE LATE 1850S, ABRAHAM LINCOLN'S REPUBLICAN

Party spent considerable time and effort cultivating the German vote in Illinois. One of Lincoln's best allies in this endeavor was his friend John Wood of Quincy, who had strong ties to the German community. Lincoln and other Republicans nominated Wood to run for lieutenant governor on the party's first statewide ticket in 1856 under William Bissell. When Bissell died in office, Wood succeeded him as governor of Illinois.

Wood was born in New York in 1798. At age 24 he settled on the banks of the Mississippi River in Illinois. A town grew up around him, which in 1825 was named the seat of Adams County and christened Quincy for President John Quincy Adams. In 1826 Wood married Ann Streeter and built a two-story log cabin farther inland from the river.

John Wood   Ann Streeter Wood

By 1835, land speculation had made Wood a wealthy man. With a growing family to accommodate, Wood had plans drawn for a grand, 14-room, Greek Revival mansion and personally selected the trees from which the timbers would be hewn and the columns turned. Wood then recruited skilled German craftsmen from St. Louis to move to Quincy and work on his house. He paid for their services by selling them land at deep discount or giving them land out-right, leading to a large and thriving German neighborhood on the city's south side. Wood maintained close ties with these immigrants, allowing them to use his pasture to graze their cows and conversing with them in fluent German.

Wood's popularity with the German community bolstered his political career, and he was elected to seven one-year terms as Quincy's mayor between 1844 and 1856, as well as to a term in the Illinois senate in 1850. When Wood was nominated for lieutenant governor, it was because the Republicans' initial choice, German immigrant Francis Hoffman, did not meet the state's resi-dency requirement. It was thought that Wood's place on the ticket might help to shore up support with German voters. Bissell and Wood were elected by a comfortable majority.

On March 18, 1860, Bissell's death from pneumonia elevated Wood to the governorship. With the spring session of the legislature ending and business

The desk, table, and horsehair-upholstered chair in Wood's custom-built office are all original to the house.

interests drawing him home, Wood was granted permission from the Illinois general assembly to remain in Quincy. He conducted business from a newly remodeled office in his private residence, which served as the executive mansion while he was governor.

Wood declined the opportunity to run for an additional term as governor at the end of Bissell's term. In 1861 he was appointed quarter master general for the state of Illinois, and in 1864 he became colonel of the 137th Illinois Regiment. By this time, Wood was a widower living in an extravagant, $200,000, octagon-shaped mansion on his estate. The old Greek Revival house had been cut in half, moved to the east side of 12th Street (its current location), and reassembled for use as the residence of Wood's grown son Daniel.

After Wood suffered financial downturn in the Panic of 1873, he sold the octagonal house and moved back into the Greek Revival house with Daniel. Daniel sold the property after his father's death in 1880, and the mansion was used as a boardinghouse for more than 20 years. In 1906 the Historical Society of Quincy and Adams County purchased the house to save it from destruction. This organization maintains and interprets the house to this day.

Visitors to the John Wood mansion will see rooms meticulously restored to their pre–Civil War appearance and filled with many Wood family objects, including the governor's hat, cane, lap desk, sofa, and decanter set, as well as an array of dresses belonging to Ann. Also on view is a table that once belonged to Quincy residents Orville and Eliza Browning. Lincoln ate at this table on October 13, 1858, while a guest of the Brownings, prior to his sixth debate with Stephen A. Douglas.

When Abraham Lincoln accepted the Republican Party's nomination for president in May 1860, Wood offered him use of the governor's office in the state capitol. Lincoln accepted and used that room as his headquarters throughout the presidential campaign.

Between court cases, Lincoln and his fellow lawyers gathered in the lobby of the William Watson Hotel.

Visit the William Watson Hotel at 105 East Washington Street, Pittsfield.

ALTHOUGH PIKE COUNTY WAS NEVER PART OF THE EIGHTH

Judicial Circuit, Abraham Lincoln's legal practice took him to Pittsfield, the county seat, for more than a dozen cases. Between sessions of court or while waiting for a verdict, Lincoln could often be found relaxing in the lobby of William Watson's Mansion House Hotel, directly across the street from the courthouse.

William Watson was born in Pennsylvania in 1798 and came to Pittsfield in 1833. In 1838, he opened the two-story, brick hotel on the south side of the public square, anticipating that the new courthouse under construction would bring increased business to Pittsfield.

In antebellum Illinois, the circuit court judge would arrive with an entourage of lawyers to hold court in each county seat twice a year. These "court weeks" had the air of a holiday for the people of the county, who flocked to town to get news, transact business, listen to the trials, and hear political speeches. In the evenings, lawyers, jurors, clients, and townspeople crowded into the local hotel or tavern to drink, play cards, share stories, and tell jokes. The Mansion House Hotel was just such a meeting place. Lincoln, Milton Hay, Stephen A. Douglas, Ozias Hatch, and other lawyers would gather in the lobby to socialize and make business connections with the local townspeople.

Watson sold the Mansion House Hotel to Joel Pennington around 1852.

William Watson

Watson built his hotel on the south side of Pittsfield's town square in 1838.

The new Pike County Courthouse was completed in 1839.

The hotel remained in business largely unchanged until around 1930, when, over strenuous local objections, its name was changed to the Parkway Hotel. In the 1950s the building became the Parkway Apartments.

In 2006 Jonas and Jane Ann Petty purchased the building with the hopes of restoring it to its 19th-century glory. Over the next two years they gutted the structure and did a complete rehabilitation. The William Watson Hotel reopened as a boutique inn, featuring original exposed brick throughout its 14 guest rooms, lobby, and breakfast room. The lobby retains one of the fireplaces that Lincoln and his colleagues used to gather around.

The William Watson Hotel reopened to the public in 2008.

20. TROBAUGH-GOOD HOUSE (HOMESTEAD PRAIRIE FARM)

The Trobaugh-Good House was a typical farmer's residence in Lincoln-era Illinois.

Visit the Trobaugh-Good House, also known as the Homestead Prairie Farm, at the Rock Springs Conservation Area, 3939 Nearing Lane, Decatur.

AS FAR AS ANYONE KNOWS, ABRAHAM LINCOLN NEVER MET

Joseph Trobaugh. Yet ordinary farmers like Trobaugh are an important part of Lincoln's story. They were the people Lincoln rubbed elbows with in stores, spoke to on the stump, and represented in court. Lincoln might have even been one of them, had he continued on the path set for him by his father.

The historical record on Trobaugh is scant: little more than a line in the 1860 census. Trobaugh was born in Tennessee around 1815. In 1853 he moved to a one-room log cabin in Macon County, Illinois, where he farmed and operated a sawmill. By 1860 he had added a room to the cabin, which now housed his mother, his wife, his three children, and two laborers.

Trobaugh was one of the tens of thousands of settlers who moved to Illinois in the years before the Civil War to take advantage of the availability of cheap, fertile land. In the young American republic, acquisition of land was the main avenue of personal advancement, particularly for people without much formal education. By buying and developing land, upwardly mobile families could enter or solidify their position in the middle class.

Lincoln's early life shared similarities with Trobaugh's. Lincoln's father, too, moved progressively westward in search of good land on which to support himself and his family, finally settling in Illinois when Lincoln was 21. Lincoln was, as he put it, "raised to farm work" in his father's home; until he came of age he engaged in the same agricultural labor that Trobaugh no doubt undertook on his farm: splitting rails, busting sod, and planting and harvesting corn.

Even after Lincoln became a lawyer, farm work continued to support his livelihood, albeit indirectly. More than three-quarters of the citizens in antebellum Illinois lived on farms, and farmers made up a good portion of Lincoln's legal clientele. They sought his services when the circuit court convened in their county each spring and fall to litigate disputes over titles, settle estates, sue for damage done to property, or recover debts. Much of Lincoln's professional income came from representing men like Trobaugh in the county courts.

Many farmers traveled to the county seat when the circuit court was in session. In addition to offering opportunities to see to legal affairs, court

FARM LANDS FOR SALE.

THE ILLINOIS CENTRAL RAILROAD COMPANY

Is now prepared to Sell

OVER TWO MILLIONS OF ACRES

OF

PRAIRIE FARM LANDS,

In Tracts of 40 Acres or upward,

ON LONG CREDITS AND AT LOW RATES OF INTEREST!

Buying land was seen as a means to social and economic advancement in antebellum America.

days were times to transact business, visit with friends, and listen to political speeches. Often farmers would attend court for the entertainment value. Although Lincoln never represented Trobaugh, it is possible that Trobaugh saw him arguing cases before the Macon County Circuit Court.

Joseph Trobaugh's homestead is the oldest surviving house in Macon County. A modest frame-covered log dwelling, it is typical of the types of houses that dotted the landscape when Lincoln rode the circuit. The Macon County Conservation District owns and interprets the house, which takes its name from Trobaugh and the subsequent owner, Emanuel Good. The homestead has been restored to its circa-1860 appearance and furnished with period antiques. Its grounds include a kitchen garden and a smokehouse that dates to the 1840s. Guided tours and living history events interpret rural life in antebellum Macon County, giving visitors the opportunity to step into the past and experience daily life in rural antebellum Illinois.

The Macon County Courthouse as it looked when Lincoln practiced there.

The restored kitchen of the Trobaugh-Good House.

An heirloom garden features plant varieties common to 1860s kitchen gardens in Illinois.

21. WILLIAM REDDICK MANSION

Spectators sat on the steps of the William Reddick Mansion to watch the first Lincoln-Douglas debate.

Visit the William Reddick Mansion at 100 West Lafayette Street, Ottawa.

ON AUGUST 21, 1858, ABRAHAM LINCOLN STOOD BEFORE A

boisterous crowd in the center of Ottawa and addressed Stephen A. Douglas in what was to become the first of the seven Lincoln-Douglas debates. Twelve thousand people braved clouds of dust and unrelenting heat to hear Lincoln and Douglas argue over how the issue of slavery would shape the nation's future.

Of the buildings that formed the perimeter of the Ottawa town square in 1858, only one still stands. The William Reddick mansion, a tall, red-brick Italianate residence, was brand new when Lincoln saw it across the square. Debate spectators crowded the stairs leading up to the imposing front entry, while Reddick's guests looked on from the upstairs balcony. Reddick himself had a prime view of the debates: he was seated on the speakers' platform at the invitation of Stephen A. Douglas.

William Reddick was born in Ireland in 1812 and came with his family to America in 1816. As a teenager, Reddick was indentured to a glass blower in Virginia. After fulfilling the terms of his contract, he removed to Pennsylvania, where he met and married Eliza Collins and established himself in the glassblowing profession.

In 1835 William and Eliza removed to Ottawa, Illinois. They were part of a large wave of migrants who moved to Illinois seeking the economic independence that came from owning land. Reddick quickly established himself in the fledgling community as a gentleman of good character. In 1838 he was

William Reddick

Pictured here in the 1860s, the Reddick Mansion was one of the most expensive and ornate private residences in the Midwest.

elected sheriff of Ottawa, a post he held until 1846, when he was elected to the Illinois senate. A staunch Democrat, Reddick did not move in the same political circles as Abraham Lincoln.

By the 1850s Reddick was a wealthy man with several business interests in town and a talent for land speculation. In 1855 he hired architects William B. Olmstead and Peter A. Nicholson to design a house befitting his wealth and social status. Construction of the 22-room, four-story Italianate mansion began in the spring of 1856. By the time the mansion was finished at a cost of nearly $25,000 in 1858, it was considered one of the most ornate and expensive residences in the Midwest. Its interior featured elaborate trim, fine furnishings, wall-to-wall carpeting, and gas chandeliers.

The Reddicks occupied the mansion until their deaths. Eliza passed away in 1883, William in 1885, and their adopted daughter Elizabeth in 1887. In 1889, per the instructions in William's will, the Reddick mansion was opened to the city of Ottawa as a public library. It served in that capacity until 1974, when the mansion was deeded to the city, and the Reddick Mansion Association was chartered to oversee the restoration, maintenance, and interpretation of the property.

The Reddicks' parlor as it appeared in the 1880s.

Today the Reddick Mansion has been restored to its 1850s appearance. It boasts wonderful examples of original plasterwork, French plate-glass windows, hand-carved Italian marble fireplaces, and trompe l'oeil faux painting. The fine collection of mid-19th-century antique furnishings includes an astronomical grandfather clock in the front hallway and a large pier mirror in the vestibule. A sofa on the second floor once belonged to the Catlin family of Ottawa, who were Lincoln's friends and political allies. Tradition has it that Abraham Lincoln sat on this sofa when he visited the Catlins.

The Reddicks' chair and ottoman grace the restored formal parlor.

22. BRYANT COTTAGE STATE HISTORIC SITE

Tradition has it that Abraham Lincoln and Stephen Douglas met at the Bryant cottage to plan the Lincoln-Douglas debates.

Visit the Bryant Cottage State Historic Site at 146 East Wilson Street, Bement.

ACCORDING TO BRYANT FAMILY TRADITION, THE COURSE OF

history was forever altered in the home of Piatt County merchant Francis Bryant on July 29, 1858. In his humble parlor, Abraham Lincoln and Stephen A. Douglas laid out the terms for a series of debates that would launch Lincoln to national prominence and ultimately help him to capture the White House two years later.

Bryant's home was built in 1856. At the time it was one of seven houses in the fledgling village of Bement. Although it had only four rooms, the cottage nonetheless boasted genteel finishes such as carpeting and wallpaper, suggesting that Bryant and his family were accustomed to comfortable living.

A prosperous businessman and a staunch Democrat, Bryant was a political ally and personal friend of Douglas. When Douglas scheduled a speech in nearby Monticello during his reelection campaign for the U.S. Senate in July of 1858, Bryant invited him to spend the night at his house.

Douglas had spent the summer on the campaign trail, drawing immense crowds at each stop. A shrewd politician and brilliant orator, Douglas was then at the height of his political powers. Lincoln admitted that Douglas enjoyed "world-wide renown" and was already being talked about as a candidate for president of the United States. Lincoln, by contrast, was a private citizen with meager prior political experience and only moderate name recognition. As Douglas stumped, Lincoln followed in his wake, taking advantage of the crowds Douglas drew to offer his own public rebuttals of Douglas's politics.

Francis Bryant

On July 24 Lincoln wrote Douglas to suggest that they "divide time, and address the same audiences during the present canvass." Douglas replied the same day, declining to share the stage at speaking arrangements he had already lined up but offering to debate Lincoln once in each of the state's congressional districts. Lincoln composed a reply to Douglas and traveled to Piatt County to deliver the letter in person on July 29.

Douglas and Lincoln met by chance on the road two miles outside Monticello. After conferring briefly, Douglas urged Lincoln to meet with him later in Bement, where he was staying. According to Bryant's descendants, Lincoln and Douglas met later that evening in the parlor of the Bryant

Stephen A. Douglas

Bement, Piatt Co. Ill.,
July 30th, 1858

Dear Sir,

Your letter, dated yesterday, accepting my proposition for a joint discussion at one prominent point in each Congressional district as stated in my previous letter was received this morning.

The times and places designated are as follows:

Ottowa, Lasalle Co.   August 21st 1858
Freeport, Stevenson Co.   "   27th   "
Jonesboro, Union Co.   September 15.   "
Charleston, Coles Co.   "   18 .   "
Galesburg, Knox Co.   October 7 .   "
Quincy, Adams Co.   "   13 .   "
Alton, Madison Co.   "   15 .   "

I agree to your suggestion that we shall alternately open and close the discussion. I will speak at Ottowa one hour, you can reply occupying an hour and a half and I will then follow for half an hour. At Freeport you shall open the discussion and speak one hour, I will follow for an hour and a half and you can then reply for half an hour. We will alternate in like manner at each successive place.

Very resp'y
Yr ob't Serv't,
S. A. Douglas

Hon. A. Lincoln,
Springfield,
Ill.

Stephen A. Douglas wrote Lincoln this letter confirming the dates and locations of the seven debates.

cottage to discuss the details of the proposed series of debates. Lincoln then took the midnight Great Western Railroad train home to Springfield; Douglas spent the night in Bement with the Bryants. Douglas wrote to Lincoln the next day, confirming the dates and locations of the seven debates. This letter bears a dateline from Bement and may well have been written at the Bryant cottage.

Per the agreement they reached, Lincoln and Douglas appeared at a series of seven joint debates in Ottawa, Freeport, Jonesboro, Charleston, Galesburg, Quincy, and Alton throughout the late summer and early fall of 1858. The main issue under consideration was the expansion of slavery. Douglas championed his notion of popular sovereignty, arguing that each state and territory should decide for itself whether to permit

Stephen A. Douglas may have stayed in this bedroom after meeting with Lincoln.

slavery. Lincoln argued that the spread of slavery must be curtailed. Although Lincoln ultimately lost his bid for the Senate, the debates garnered national attention and helped pave the way for Lincoln's nomination as the Republican candidate for president of the United States in 1860.

Today the Bryant Cottage State Historic Site is owned by the state of Illinois. Several Bryant family furnishings are on display, including a "yarn weasel" and the horsehair-upholstered parlor suite. Along with the kitchen and sitting room, visitors may view the bedroom in which Douglas might have stayed when he spent the night with the Bryants in 1858, as well as the parlor where Lincoln and Douglas sat to plan their series of historic debates.

RELATED LINCOLN SITES

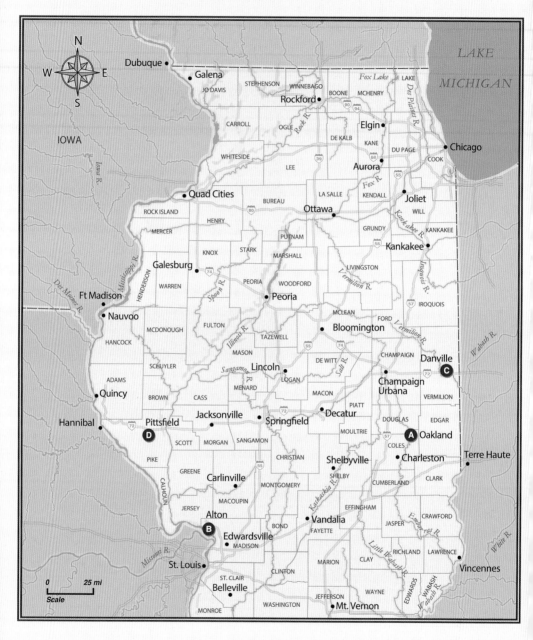

A. HIRAM RUTHERFORD HOUSE

14 South Pike Street, Oakland, IL 61943

Hiram Rutherford was a Coles County abolitionist who helped a family of African American slaves escape their master in Coles County, Illinois; Abraham Lincoln was involved in the lawsuits that resulted from Rutherford's aid to fugitive slaves.

In 1847 slaveholder Robert Matson often brought slaves up from his Kentucky plantation to work on his Coles County farm. While working in Illinois, one of these enslaved woman, Jane Bryant, heard that Matson was planning to sell her and her children when they returned to Kentucky. Desperate, she took her children and fled to the protection of local abolitionists Gideon Ashmore and Hiram Rutherford. Matson sued Ashmore and Rutherford for $2,500 in damages for having taken his human "property." Rutherford tried to hire Lincoln to represent him at trial, but Lincoln had already committed to represent Matson. After the court ruled in favor of Ashmore and Rutherford, the Bryant family removed to Monrovia, Liberia.

Rutherford's house, built in 1847, still survives in Oakland, along with the adjacent office he built in 1855. Rutherford lived in his home until his death in 1900. The site was placed on the National Register of Historic Places in 1982 and is now part of the Oakland Historic Landmarks.

B. LYMAN TRUMBULL HOUSE

1105 Henry Avenue, Alton, IL 62002

Lyman Trumbull was an old friend and political rival-turned-ally of Abraham Lincoln. The two men likely first met while serving in the Illinois House of Representatives in 1840. After a brief flirtation with Mary Todd ("he is talented & agreeable & sometimes *countenances* me," Mary wrote in 1841), Trumbull married Mary's friend and bridesmaid Julia Jayne in 1843.

Trumbull got his start in Illinois politics as a Democrat, serving successively as a state representative, secretary of state, and justice of the Illinois Supreme Court. In 1854 Trumbull defeated Lincoln for a seat in the U.S. Senate. (Mary Lincoln never forgave Julia Trumbull for this perceived betrayal.) Trumbull later supported Lincoln's unsuccessful bid for the Senate in 1858 and his candidacy for the presidency in 1860.

During Lincoln's administration, the relationship between the two men cooled as Trumbull found more in common with the radical wing of the

Republican Party. In 1865 Trumbull coauthored the 13th Amendment, abolishing slavery, which Lincoln heartily supported.

Trumbull's one-and-a-half story, gable-roofed residence survives on Henry Avenue in Alton, Illinois. Built between 1820 and 1837, it was home to Trumbull and his family from 1849 to 1863. It was added to the National Register of Historic Places in 1975. Today it is a private dwelling.

C. LAMON HOUSE

1031 North Logan Avenue, Danville, IL 61832

In 1855 Joseph and Melissa Lamon hired Abraham Lincoln as their attorney to appeal a settlement from the Great Western Railroad for damage done to their property. They might have been acquainted with him through Joseph's cousin, Ward Hill Lamon, with whom Lincoln often collaborated on cases when he was in Danville. Lincoln pled the case successfully, and the court increased the Lamons' award.

The house where Joseph and Melissa Lamon lived still stands in Danville. Built in the 1840s, it is thought to be the oldest frame house in the city. Today it is owned by the Vermilion County Museum, which undertook an extensive renovation of the home in 1984, and is open to the public for tours.

D. ABE LINCOLN TALKING HOUSES TOUR

Pittsfield, Illinois

Several sites associated with Lincoln survive in Pittsfield; these have been organized into a car audio tour that provides information about each site and its Lincoln connection. Sites on the tour include

1. Milton Hay House, 332 West Washington Street: The home of Lincoln's friend and legal associate Milton Hay and his nephew, John Hay, who later became one of President Lincoln's private secretaries.
2. Reuben Scanland House, 402 West Washington Street: Abraham Lincoln spent the night here in October of 1858.
3. William Grimshaw House, 1000 West Perry Street: Attorney William Grimshaw worked with Lincoln on several Pike County court cases.
4. Site of Daniel H. Gilmer House, corner of Washington and Monroe Streets: Lincoln was a frequent visitor to Gilmer's home.
5. Charles Lame House, 409 East Fayette Street: Lincoln visited Lame at his home after Lame was injured in the test firing of a cannon during the Lincoln 1858 senatorial campaign.

6. Michael J. Noyes House, 629 East Washington Street: Lincoln is said to have given a speech on the front lawn of this house.
7. Colonel William Ross House, Illinois Route 106: Lincoln reportedly stayed here while campaigning for the Senate in 1858.
8. Zachariah N. Garbutt House, 500 East Washington Street: One of Lincoln's presidential secretaries, John G. Nicolay, lived in this house for seven years as a printer's apprentice.
9. The Star Hotel, corner of Monroe and Jefferson Streets: Abraham Lincoln is said to have stayed here while visiting Pittsfield.
10. Site of Joseph Heck Bakery, corner of Madison and Adams Streets: John G. Nicolay took Lincoln to Heck's bakery for cider and gingerbread on October 1, 1858.

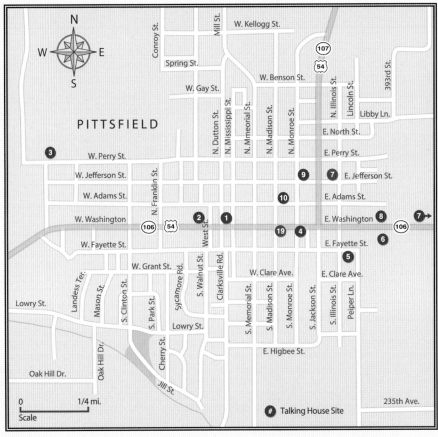

Numbers in red circles indicate sites on the talking houses tour. Numbers in blue circles represent sites described in part 2 (Shastid House, 7) and part 3 (William Watson Hotel, 19).

FOR FURTHER READING
ILLUSTRATION CREDITS
INDEX

FOR FURTHER READING

Andreasen, Bryon. *Looking for Lincoln in Illinois: Lincoln and Mormon Country*. Carbondale: Southern Illinois University Press, 2015.

———. *Looking for Lincoln in Illinois: Lincoln's Springfield*. Carbondale: Southern Illinois University Press, 2015.

Bartlett, D. W. *The Life and Public Services of Hon. Abraham Lincoln*. New York: H. Dayton, 1860.

Berry, Stephen. *House of Abraham: Lincoln and the Todds, a Family Divided by War*. Boston: Mariner Books, 2009.

Burlingame, Michael. *Abraham Lincoln Traveled This Way: The America Lincoln Knew*. Heyworth, IL: Firelight Publishing, 2011.

Coleman, Charles H. *Abraham Lincoln in Coles County, Illinois*. New Brunswick, NJ: Scarecrow Press, 1955.

Edgar County Historical Society. *Memoirs of Abraham Lincoln in Edgar County*. 1925.

Faragher, John Mack. *Sugar Creek: Life on the Illinois Prairie*. New Haven: Yale University Press, 1986.

Fraker, Guy C. *Lincoln's Ladder to the Presidency: The Eighth Judicial Circuit*. Carbondale: Southern Illinois University Press, 2012.

———. *Looking for Lincoln in Illinois: A Guide to Lincoln's Eighth Judicial Circuit*. Carbondale: Southern Illinois University Press, 2017.

Gary, Ralph V. *Following in Lincoln's Footsteps: A Complete Annotated Reference to Hundreds of Historical Sites Visited by Abraham Lincoln*. New York: Basic Books, 2002.

Grant, Helen Hardie. *Peter Cartwright: Pioneer*. New York: Abington Press, 1931.

Guelzo, Allen. *Lincoln and Douglas: The Debates That Defined America*. New York: Simon and Schuster, 2008.

Holst, Erika. *Edwards Place: A Springfield Treasure*. Springfield, IL: Springfield Art Association, 2015.

King, Willard. *Lincoln's Manager, David Davis*. Cambridge: Harvard University Press, 1960.

Lincoln, Abraham. *The Collected Works of Abraham Lincoln*, edited by Roy P. Basler. 9 vols. New Brunswick, NJ: Rutgers University Press, 1953–55.

Masters, Edgar Lee. *Vachel Lindsay: A Poet in America*. New York: Biblo and Tannen, 1969.

Plummer, Mark. *Lincoln's Rail-Splitter, Governor Richard J. Oglesby*. Urbana: University of Illinois Press, 2001.

Putnam, Elizabeth Duncan. *Life and Services of Joseph Duncan: Governor of Illinois, 1834–1848*. Springfield, IL: Reprinted from *Transactions of the Illinois State Historical Society*, 1921.

Raymond, Mary, ed. *Some Incidents in the Life of Mrs. Benjamin S. Edwards*. Springfield, IL: privately published, 1909.

Sandburg, Carl. *Abraham Lincoln: The Prairie Years and the War Years*. New York: Mariner Books, 2002.

Shastid, Thomas H. *My Second Life*. Ann Arbor: George Wahr, publisher to the University of Michigan, 1944.

Stuart-Hay Papers. Abraham Lincoln Presidential Library.

Temple, Wayne C. *By Square and Compass: The Saga of Lincoln's Home*. Rev. ed. Mahomet, IL: Mayhaven Publishing, 2002.

Thomas, Benjamin P. *Lincoln's New Salem*. Springfield, IL: Abraham Lincoln Association, 1934.

Turner, Glennette Tilley. *The Underground Railroad in Illinois*. Wheaton, IL: Newman Educational Publishing, 2001.

Turner, Justin G., and Linda Levitt Turner. *Mary Todd Lincoln: Her Life and Letters*. New York: Fromm International, 1987.

Wilson, Douglas L., and Rodney O. Davis, eds. *Herndon's Informants: Letters, Interviews, and Statements about Abraham Lincoln*. Urbana: University of Illinois Press, 1997.

Yoder, Paton. *Taverns and Travelers: Inns of the Early Midwest*. Bloomington: Indiana University Press, 1969.

ILLUSTRATION CREDITS

Modern Images

Most of the modern images in this book were photographed by the author. The exceptions are the David Davis Mansion State Historic Site images, which were provided by the David Davis Mansion Foundation; the Lincoln Home National Historic Site images, which were provided by the National Park Service; the Edwards Place images, which were taken by Anastasia Lowenthal and provided courtesy of the Springfield Art Association; and the modern interior images of the Joseph Smith Mansion House and Homestead, which were taken by Val Brinkerhoff and provided courtesy of the Community of Christ.

All maps were created by Tom Willcockson, Mapcraft Custom Cartography.

Historical Images

Most of the historical images in this book are courtesy of the Abraham Lincoln Presidential Library and Museum. The rest came from the following sources.

INSTITUTIONAL REPOSITORIES

- Abraham Lincoln Library and Museum, Harrogate, Tennessee. Page 8, Thomas Lincoln. Courtesy of Abraham Lincoln Library and Museum, Harrogate, Tennessee.
- Bryant Cottage State Historic Site, Bement, Illinois. Page 95, Francis Bryant.
- Elijah Iles House Foundation. Page 30, Robert Irwin.
- Historical Society of Quincy and Adams County, Quincy, Illinois. Page 76, Quincy, circa 1850. Page 74, Richard Eells house.
- Library of Congress. Page 96, Stephen Douglas to Abraham Lincoln, July 30, 1858.
- Paris Bicentennial Art Center and Museum, Paris, Illinois. Page 52, Milton K. Alexander Home.
- Pike County Historical Society, Pittsfield, Illinois. Page 83, Mansion House Hotel.

- Pleasant Plains Historical Society, Pleasant Plains, Illinois. Page 64, Broadwell Inn overgrown.
- Reddick Mansion, Ottawa, Illinois. Page 91, historic exterior of Reddick Mansion. Page 92, historic interior of Reddick Mansion. Page 91, William Reddick.
- Springfield Art Association, Springfield, Illinois. Page 24, Benjamin Edwards. Page 25, Helen Edwards. Page 26, historic exterior of Edwards Place.
- Vermilion County Museum, Danville, Illinois. Page 50, Fithian Home, circa 1890.
- Vespasian Warner Public Library District Special Collections, Clinton, Illinois. Page 45, book flyleaf with Lincoln's handwriting.

PUBLIC DOMAIN PUBLICATIONS

- Library of Congress; published by H. M. Clay, March 13, 1861, Buffalo, N.Y.; lithographer, J. Sage and Sons. Page 33, quail.
- *History of Pike County, Illinois*. Chicago: Charles C. Chapman and Company, 1880, pp. 190, 655. Page 84, Pike County Courthouse. Page 83, William Watson.
- Illinois Central Railroad, 1855. Page 87, land sale broadside.
- Shastid, Thomas Hall. *Tramping to Failure*. Ann Arbor, MI: George Wahr, 1937, pp. 17–18. Page 33, John G. Shastid. Page 34, Thomas W. Shastid.
- Stevens, Frank E. *The Black Hawk War*. Chicago: Frank E. Stevens, 1903, p. 192. Page 52, Milton K. Alexander.

INDEX

Page numbers in italics indicate illustrations.

Star Hotel, Pittsfield, 101
Streeter, Ann, 78

13th Amendment to U.S. Constitution, 37, 99
Todd, John, 59
Todd, Mary. *See* Lincoln, Mary Todd
Trobaugh, Joseph, 57, 86–87
Trobaugh-Good House (Homestead Prairie Farm), Decatur, 57, 86–89, *86*, *89*
Trumbull, Lyman, 99–100
Trumbull House, Alton, 99–100

U.S. Constitution, 13th Amendment, 37, 99

Vachel Lindsay Home State Historic Site, Springfield, 3, *13* (map), 18–21, *18*, *21*
Vermilion County Museum, Danville, *48*, 49–50, 100

Walker, Sarah, 41
Watson, William, *83*
Watson Hotel (formerly Mansion House Hotel), Pittsfield, 57, 82–85, *82*, *83*, *85*
Whig party, in Illinois, 58
William Grinshaw House, Pittsfield, 101
William Reddick Mansion, Ottawa, 57, 90–93, *90*, *91*, *92*, *93*
William Ross House, Pittsfield, 101
William Watson Hotel (formerly Mansion House Hotel), Pittsfield, 57, 82–85, *82*, *83*, *85*
Wood, Ann Streeter, 78, *79*
Wood, Daniel, 80
Wood, John, 78–79, *79*
Wood Mansion, Quincy, 78–81

Zachariah N. Garbutt House, Pittsfield, 101

ERIKA HOLST is the curator of decorative arts and history at the Illinois State Museum. Her previous publications include *Wicked Springfield: Crime, Corruption, and Scandal during the Lincoln Era* and *Edwards Place: A Springfield Treasure.*

LOOKING FOR LINCOLN HERITAGE COALITION